Granny Squares Weekend

20 quick and easy crochet projects

EMMA VARNAM

THE GUILD OF MASTER CRAFTSMAN PUBLICATIONS

First published 2018 by
Guild of Master Craftsman Publications Ltd
Castle Place, 166 High Street, Lewes,
East Sussex BN7 1XU, UK

Reprinted 2019

ISBN 978 1 78494 384 4

A catalogue record for this book is available from
the British Library.

Publisher: Jonathan Bailey
Production Manager: Jim Bulley
Senior Project Editor: Wendy McAngus
Editor: Nicola Hodgson
Managing Art Editor: Gilda Pacitti
Designer: Manisha Patel
Photographer: Emma Sekhon
Illustrator: Martin Woodward

Colour origination by GMC Reprographics
Printed and bound in China

Contents

Introduction

I cannot think of anything more delightful than a weekend spent curling up on the sofa with my yarn and hook, crocheting something cosy. For this book, I have designed patterns that are based around the classic granny square, but with a modern twist.

These projects will not take you long to make. They are quick and easy to complete once you know the basics of crochet, so you should be able to complete them in a weekend. And the items themselves are intended to be used while you are relaxing.

Many of the projects, including the Perfect Potholder, the Fingerless Mittens and the Panda Comforter, make excellent gifts. If you are visiting friends at the weekend, you could whip them up a personalized gift instead of taking a bottle or flowers. Even better, take all three.

Patterns such as the Glasses Case and the Lazy-edged Blanket are ones that I make again and again, as they are both practical and attractive.

Throughout the book you will find hints and tips that I hope will improve your crochet technique. I have tried to give you help and knowledge that will allow you to avoid the mistakes I have made over the years.

Crochet is a wonderfully relaxing hobby, providing a perfect distraction from the stresses of work, study and a busy life, while also being practical. Let crochet help soothe away your concerns as you take some time off this weekend.

BOLSTER CUSHION
page 104

DRAUGHT
EXCLUDER
page 92

SMART
DOORSTOP
page 84

STYLISH TABLEMAT
page 76

GLASSES CASE
page 80

FESTIVAL
BAG
page 120

FINGERLESS
MITTENS
page 124

FLOWER HEADBAND
page 64

STRIPED BERET
page 136

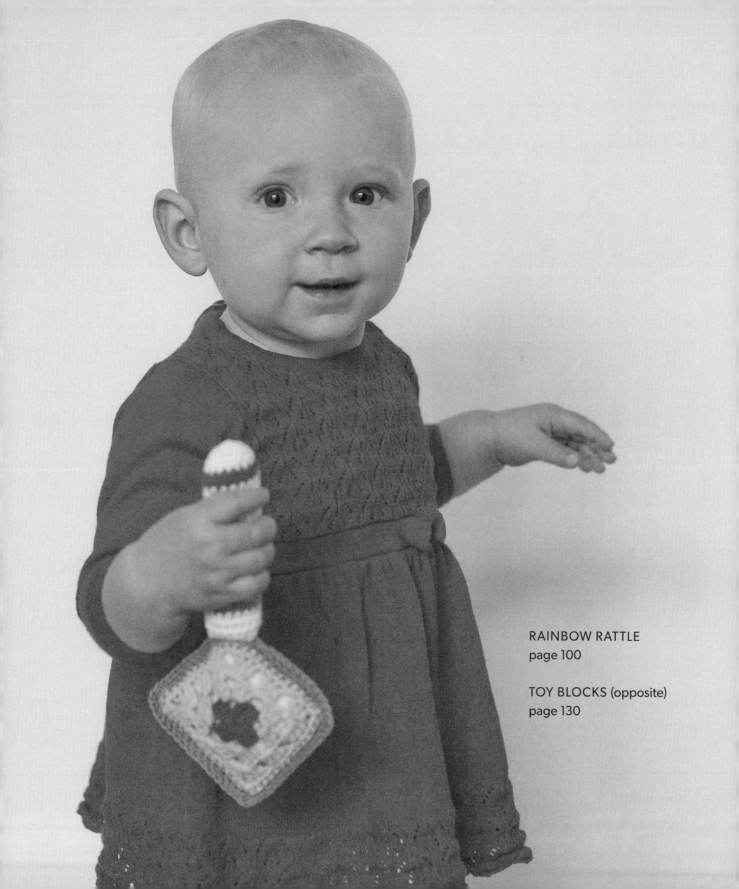

RAINBOW RATTLE
page 100

TOY BLOCKS (opposite)
page 130

PANDA COMFORTER
page 116

POMPOM
BUNTING
page 68

getting started

What you'll need

Crochet is worked with just one hook, so once you are equipped with that and a selection of yarn you are ready to get started.

Crochet hooks

Crochet hooks come in a range of materials and sizes. In this book, I use a wide range of sizes according to the thickness of the yarn. For size 3.5mm or 4mm I like to use an ergonomic metal-pointed crochet hook. The larger hooks, such as 8mm or 9mm, are usually made either in plastic or wood.

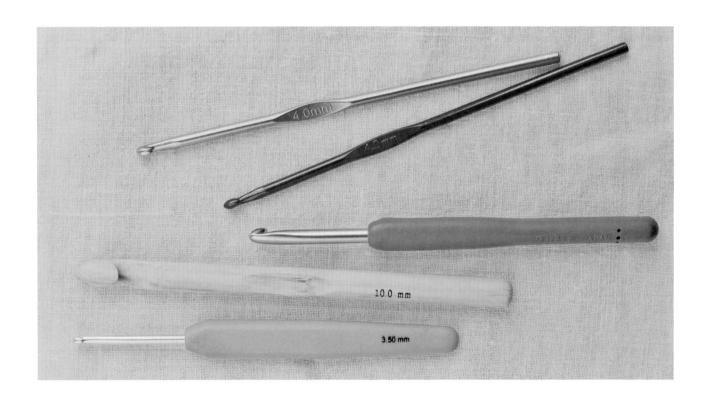

Yarn

I love working with soft, natural yarns. When I make babywear or clothes for myself, I choose the most expensive yarn I can afford. Pure wool or yarn with a cashmere fibre added to it is very luxurious and soft to the touch, but this type of yarn is for very special projects – heirloom pieces, if you like. Merino wool is ideal for soft scarves or children's garments. Yarn used for homewear or toys needs to be very hardwearing. These items are likely to get dirty and will benefit from being laundered in the washing machine.

Cotton

Cotton yarn is wonderful for toys and accessories for the garden. The colours have an appealing clarity and brightness. Cotton is also very durable and is less likely to disintegrate with extensive use. Worked tightly in close stitches, cotton forms a very firm fabric, which makes it the go-to material for many toy designers.

Acrylic yarns and mixes

Acrylic yarns have improved greatly in the past few years. They would often come in garish colours and were scratchy, but recent technology means that acrylic yarn and blends feel almost as soft as merino or cashmere. These yarns also come in a wide range of subtle and natural colours. It takes a seasoned eye to tell the difference. Acrylic yarn is made from ethylene, which is derived from oil. The yarn is robust, resistant to moths and can be washed without worry. Also, it is cheaper to manufacture yarn in this way, so buying enough to make a blanket need not break the bank.

Handy tip

Granny squares are great for using up yarn remnants, but make sure that the weight of the yarn remains the same for the whole project. Therefore, if you choose a DK yarn for a blanket, try to ensure that all the rounds or rows are worked in DK.

Handy tip

It's easy to lose count of stitches or rows – even experienced crocheters do. I don't use expensive stitch markers, I just cut a small amount of yarn, about 2in (5cm) long, and place this between the last stitch of one row and the first stitch of the next. When I have finished, these small strands can easily be pulled out without snagging the stitches.

Stuffing

I have used Minicraft Supersoft toy stuffing to stuff the Rainbow Rattle and the head of the Panda Comforter. This material complies with BS145, BN5852 and EN71 standards and is safe for children. Make sure the panda is stuffed so that it is firm but not bulging, as this will distort the facial features.

The Toy Blocks are stuffed with a cube of upholstery foam. You can buy foam at most hobby shops, and it is easy to cut using scissors. However, if you have some old play blocks, you could upcycle them by removing the old fabric covers and covering them in the crochet fabric.

Needles

You will need a variety of needles for completing the projects, including a tapestry needle for sewing in ends and adding embroidery details, and a fine beading needle for sewing on beads.

Plastic safety eyes

I used plastic safety eyes for the Panda Comforter. These come in two parts: a shank to push through the crochet, and a plastic or metal washer that fits very securely over the shank inside the head.

Once the washer has been added it is very hard to undo, so make sure you place the eyes exactly where you want them. It can be helpful to fill the head with a little stuffing to ensure that the eyes are in the right position before you attach the washer. Once you have pushed both parts of the eyes together, give them a test tug and try to pull them out to make sure they are fixed securely.

Conversions

Crochet hooks

UK	Metric	US
14	2mm	0
13	2.25mm	B/1
12	2.5mm	–
–	2.75mm	C/2
11	3mm	–
10	3.25mm	D/3
9	3.5mm	E/4
–	3.75mm	F/5
8	4mm	G/6
7	4.5mm	7
6	5mm	H/8
5	5.5mm	I/9
4	6mm	J/10
3	6.5mm	K/10.5
2	7mm	–
0	8mm	L/11
00	9mm	M–N/13
000	10mm	N–P/15

Crochet techniques

This section will explain all the basic techniques needed to make the projects in this book. Some will need a bit of practice, but with time they will become second nature.

Holding yarn

With the hand you are not using to hold the hook, wrap the yarn around your little finger and then drape the yarn over your hand. You can hold the tail of your yarn between the middle finger and your thumb and use your index finger to control the yarn.

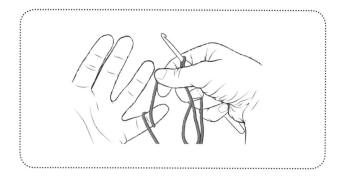

Holding a hook

Hold your hook in either your right or your left hand as you would a pen, in between your index finger and thumb.

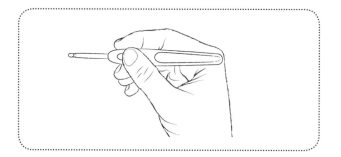

Making a slip knot

Make a loop of yarn over two fingers. Pull a second loop through this first loop, pull it up and slip it onto your crochet hook. Pull the knot gently so that it forms a loose knot on the hook.

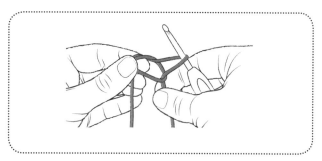

UK and US differences

Some UK and US terms have different meanings, which can cause confusion, so always check which style the pattern you are using is written in. This will ensure that your crochet develops correctly – there is nothing more frustrating than working on a pattern, then realising it is all wrong and needs to be unravelled.

UK/US crochet terms

UK	US
Double crochet	Single crochet
Half treble	Half double crochet
Treble	Double crochet
Double treble	Triple crochet
Treble treble	Double triple crochet

Note: This book uses UK crochet terms

Abbreviations

alt	alternate
ch	chain
ch sp	chain space(s)
cm	centimetres
cont	continue
dc	double crochet
dc2inc	double crochet increase by one stitch
dc2tog	double crochet two stitches together (decrease by one stitch)
dc3tog	double crochet three stitches together (decrease by two stitches)
dec	decrease
DK	double knitting
dtr	double treble
g	grams
htr	half treble
in	inch(es)
inc	increase
m	metre(s)
mm	millimetre(s)
rep	repeat
RS	right side
RtrF	raised treble front
sl st	slip stitch
sp(s)	space(s)
st(s)	stitch(es)
tbl	through the back loop
tog	together
tr	treble
WS	wrong side
yd	yard(s)
yo	yarn over

Chain stitch (ch st)

1 Start with a slip knot on the hook.

2 Wrap the yarn over the hook.

3 Pull the loop through the loop of the slip knot to form one chain stitch.

Slip stitch (sl st)

This stitch is ideal for decoration and attaching two pieces of crochet together.

1 Insert the hook into a stitch, and wrap the yarn over the hook. Draw the loop through the stitch and the loop on the hook.

2 Continue in this way for the required number of slip stitches.

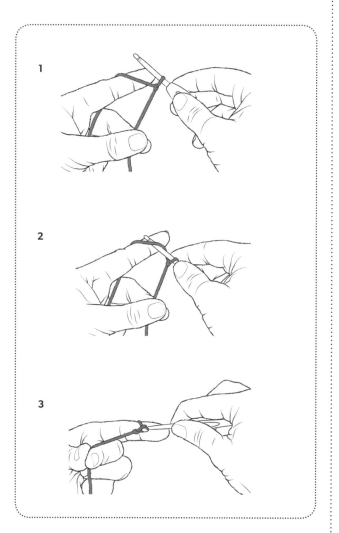

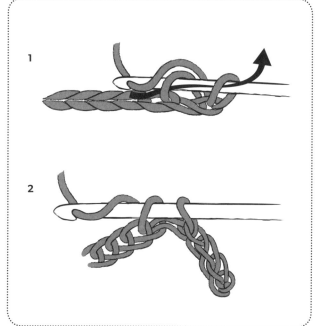

Double crochet (dc)

1 Insert the hook through the stitch, yarn over the hook, and pull through the stitch. There will be two loops on the hook.

2 Wrap the yarn over the hook and pull through both loops on the hook. There will be one loop on the hook.

Half treble crochet (htr)

1 Wrap the yarn over the hook, insert the hook through the stitch, yarn over the hook and pull through the stitch. There will be three loops on the hook.

2 Wrap the yarn over the hook again and draw through all the loops on the hook. There will be one loop on the hook.

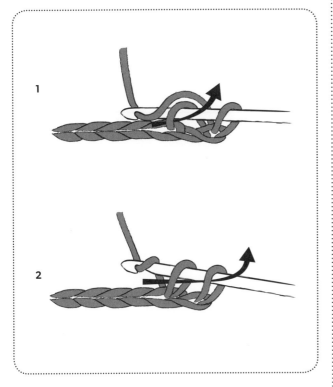

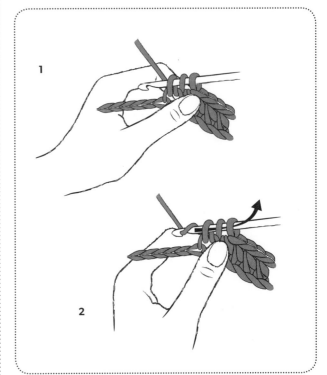

Treble crochet (tr)

1 Wrap the yarn over the hook, and insert the hook through the stitch. Wrap the yarn over the hook and pull through the stitch.

2 Wrap the yarn over the hook and pull through two loops. There will be two loops on the hook.

3 Wrap the yarn over the hook again and pull through the remaining two loops. There will be one loop left on the hook.

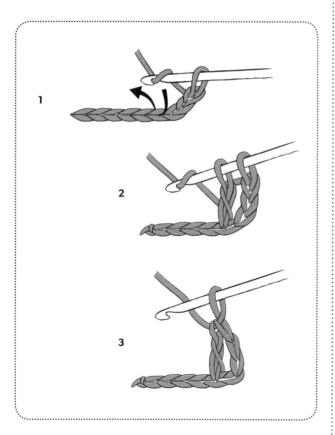

Double treble crochet (dtr)

1 Wrap the yarn over the hook twice, insert the hook through the stitch, yarn over the hook and pull through the stitch. There will be four loops on the hook.

2 Wrap the yarn over the hook and pull through two loops. There will be three loops on the hook.

3 Wrap the yarn over the hook and pull through two loops. There will be two loops on the hook.

4 Wrap the yarn over and pull through the remaining two loops. There will be one loop on the hook.

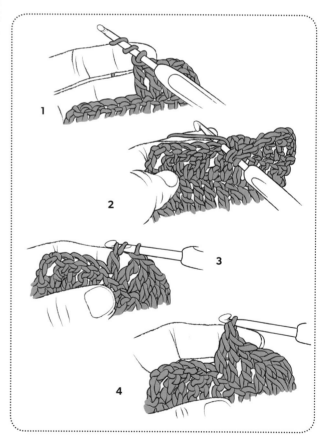

Working in rows

When making straight rows, you need to make a turning chain at the beginning of the row for the stitch you are working on. A double crochet row will need one chain at the beginning of the row; this will be indicated in the pattern.

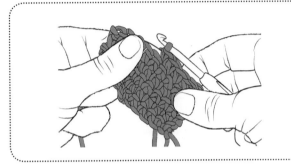

Working in rounds

One wonderful thing about crochet is that you don't always have to work in rows; you can also work in rounds. The patterns for the Cheery Coaster and the Chunky Lap Blanket start with a chain ring (see section below on Joining a ring), while the Rainbow Rattle starts with a magic ring (see page 44) and is then worked in continuous spiral rounds with no slip-stitch joins or turning chains.

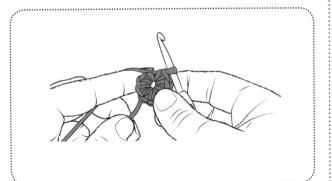

Joining a ring

1 Work the number of chain stitches specified in the instructions for your pattern.

2 Insert the hook into the first chain stitch made.

3 Wrap the yarn over the hook and pull through two stitches on the hook.

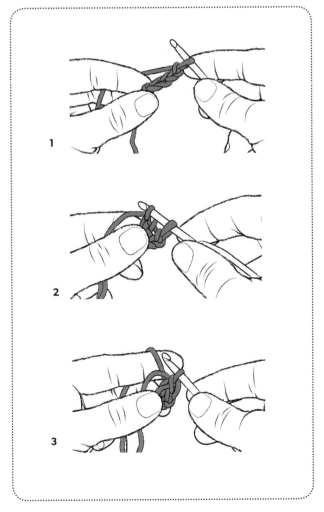

Basic granny square pattern

Granny squares are always worked from the centre outwards. The basic granny square can be worked in two ways: either starting at the beginning of the corner group, or in the middle.

Round 1: Using first colour, ch 6 sts, join with a sl st to form a ring.

Round 2: Ch 3 (this counts as the first tr), 2 tr into ring, 3 ch, *3 tr into the ring, 3 ch, rep from * twice, join the round with a sl st at the top of the first ch. Break off yarn.

Round 3: Change to second colour. Attach yarn in any corner ch sp using a sl st, 3 ch (counts as the first tr), 2 tr into same ch sp, 3 ch, 3 tr into same sp, *1 ch, miss 3 tr, (3 tr, 3 ch, 3 tr) into next ch sp, rep from * twice, 1 ch, miss 3 tr, sl st into third of 3 ch at beg of round. Fasten off.

Round 4: Change to third colour. Attach yarn in any corner chain sp using a sl st, 3 ch (counts as the first tr), 2 tr into same ch sp, 3 ch, 3 tr in same space, *1 ch, miss 3 tr, 3 tr into next ch sp, 1 ch, miss 3 tr, (3 tr, 3 ch, 3 tr) into next ch sp, rep from * twice, 1 ch, miss 3 tr, 3 tr into next ch sp, 1 ch, miss 3 tr, sl st into third of 3 ch at beg of round. Fasten off.

Crocheting into spaces

When creating a granny square, you need to work into a chain space made in the previous row, instead of working into a stitch. When you begin a row with a new colour, you join with a slip stitch working into a chain space.

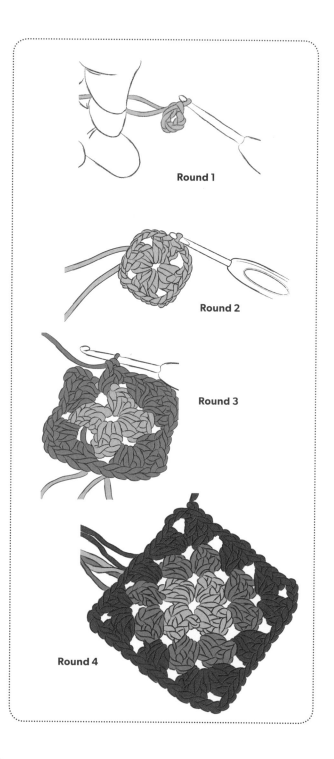

Round 1

Round 2

Round 3

Round 4

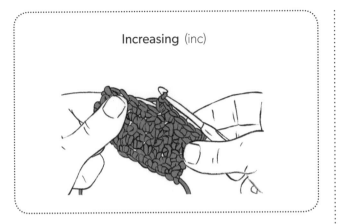

Increasing (inc)

Increasing (inc)

Work a stitch as normal, then work another into the same stitch of the previous row.

Decreasing (dc2tog)

1 Insert your hook into the next stitch, pull a loop through, insert your hook into the next stitch, and pull a loop through.

2 Wrap the yarn over the hook and pull the yarn through all three loops.

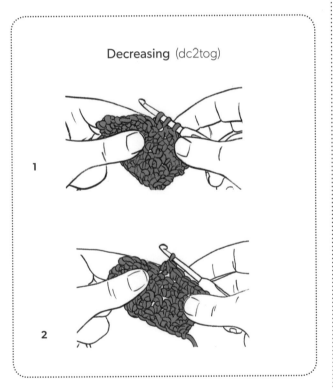

Decreasing (dc2tog)

1

2

Through back loop (tbl)

Generally, a crochet stitch is made by slipping the hook under the top two loops of a stitch. However, you can also create a different effect by working into the back loop only of each stitch of one round or row. This creates a ridge or horizontal bar across the row. In this book I have used this technique for the Stylish Tablemat, the Chunky Lap Blanket and the Striped Beret.

Magic ring

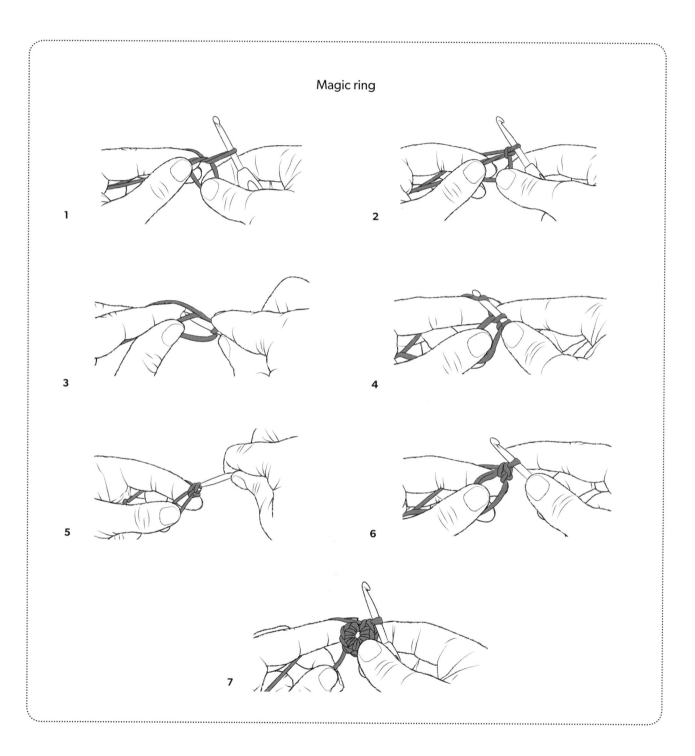

Magic ring

In recent years, with the increasing interest in making amigurumi or crochet toys, the magic ring (also known as the magic circle) technique has become popular. This is a neat way of starting a circular piece of crochet while avoiding the unsightly hole that can be left in the centre when you join a ring the normal way. Magic rings are nearly always made with double crochet stitches, as this creates a tight, dense crochet fabric. This technique is used for several projects, including the head of the Panda Comforter.

1 Start by making a basic slip knot. Pull up the loop and slip this loop onto your crochet hook.

2 Before you tighten the ring, wrap the yarn over the hook (outside the circle) and pull through to make the first chain.

3 Insert the hook into the ring, wrap the yarn over the hook and pull through the ring so there are two loops on the hook.

4 Wrap the yarn over the hook again (outside the circle) and pull through both loops.

5 You have made your first double crochet stitch.

6 Continue to work like this for as many double crochet stitches as are stated in the pattern instructions.

7 Pull the yarn tail to tighten the ring and then continue working in the round as usual.

Crab stitch

Crab stitch gives a neat finish, creating the effect of a corded edge. I have used it in the Cheery Coaster. This stitch is made by working double crochet in the opposite direction to normal; that is, from left to right. It can feel slightly awkward to work but is worth it.

1 With RS facing, insert the hook from front to back into the stitch immediately to the right of the last one. Point the hook slightly downwards and catch the yarn at the back. Bring the yarn through the stitch. Wrap the yarn around the hook and draw it through the two loops.

2 Repeat to the end of the row.

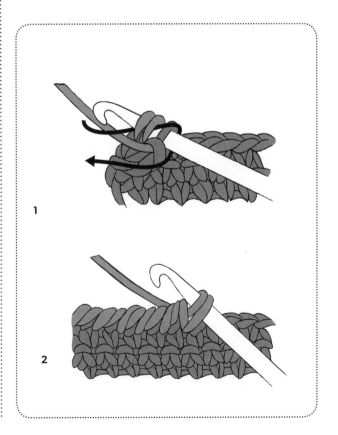

Shell stitch

A shell is made by working several stitches into a single stitch. In order to keep the rest of your work flat, you need to miss one or more base stitches in the row below.

1 Miss the number of stitches as indicated in the pattern.

2 Work 4 tr or 5 tr into the next stitch. Miss the number of stitches as indicated in the pattern.

3 Slip stitch in the next stitch. Repeat along the edge.

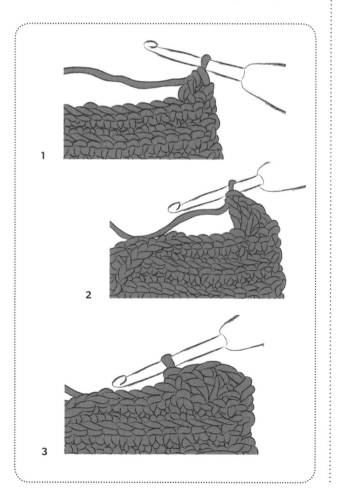

Puff stitch

One way to create texture and interest in crochet is to insert a puff stitch. A puff stitch is made by working several stitches into one stitch then gathering them all at the top.

1 Puff stitches bring together a group of half treble stitches. * Yarn around the hook, insert the hook into ch or st, pull the yarn through the work. Rep from * three times.

2 Yarn over hook and pull through all 9 loops on hook.

3 Ch 1 then work your next puff stitch into the following chain space.

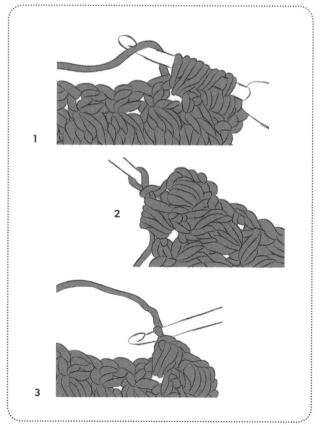

Edging fabric

The Lazy-edged Blanket requires you to add a crochet edging to a ready-made blanket. If you have a very open-weave fabric, like a natural linen, it is possible to make a spike stitch by pushing a thin crochet hook through the cloth about ½in (1.25cm) in from the edge and then completing a double crochet stitch. Continue in this way to create a foundation row around the edge.

With a dense fabric, the best idea is to sew a blanket stitch foundation for your crochet stitches by using a sewing needle and the yarn you will be using for your crochet.

Blanket stitch

1 With your edge away from you, bring your threaded needle out through the very edge of the fabric.

2 Insert your needle to the left and poke into the fabric edge as before, loop the thread under the tip of the needle and pull the needle through.

3 Make the next stitch in the same way to the left, making sure the vertical stitches are the same length and the same distance apart.

4 Once you have completed the blanket stitch edging you will have a line of yarn that sits along the outside edge of your fabric. You can now attach your yarn by slipping your crochet hook under this line and beginning with a sl st. I find that I can fit three or four double crochet stitches in between each vertical blanket stitch.

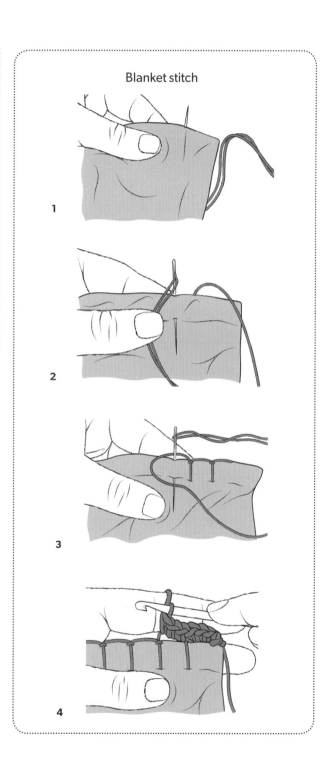

Blanket stitch

Finishing touches

This section shows you how to make up your finished project so that it is robust and durable, and how to add extra details.

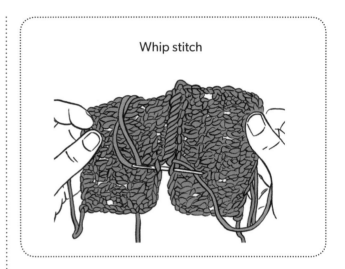

Whip stitch

Whip stitch

You can use whip stitch to sew two layers of fabric together. Make a knot at the end of your yarn. Bring your needle from the wrong side through to the right side of your fabric, then hold both pieces of your fabric together, wrong sides facing each other. Push your needle from the back piece through to the front piece, and repeat evenly along the edge. There will be a row of small stitches along the edge of your work, joining both pieces together.

Slip-stitch seam

Place the pieces of the crochet together with wrong sides facing each other. Insert the hook through both pieces at the beginning of the seam and pull up a loop, then chain one stitch. Work a row of slip stitches by inserting your hook through both sides at the same time.

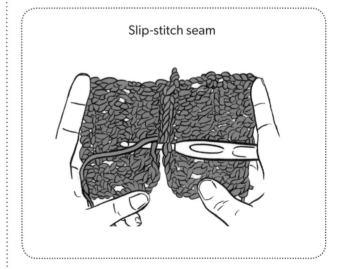

Slip-stitch seam

Double-crochet seam

Work as for a slip-stitch seam but working double crochet instead of slip stitch. If you work around a corner, work three small stitches into the corners.

Joining as you go

For the Bolster Cushion, I joined the squares together as I went along, joining the corners of the last round of each square to the adjoining and opposite corners and chain spaces of the square next to it. This allows you the build the crochet material as you work. The key is to attach each corner or chain space with a small slip stitch.

Weaving in ends

Try to leave about 8in (20cm) of yarn when you fasten off. You may be able to hide the tail in your next row. I always ensure that my ends have been woven backwards and forwards three times.

1 Thread the remaining yarn end onto a blunt tapestry needle and weave in the yarn on the wrong side of the project. Work along the stitches one way, then work back in the opposite direction.

2 Weave the needle behind the first ridge of crochet for at least 2in (5cm). Snip off the end of the yarn close to the fabric of the crochet.

Handy tip

If you dread weaving in ends try breaking up the chore into manageable chunks to make it less daunting.

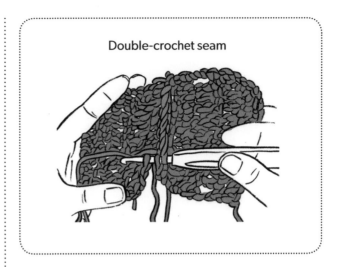

Double-crochet seam

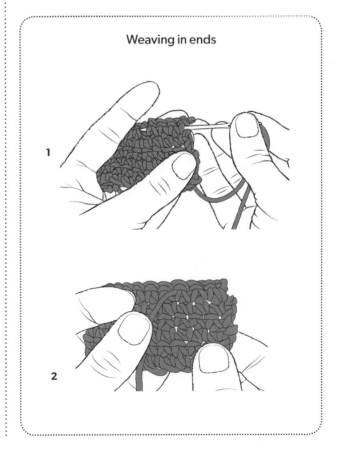

Weaving in ends

1

2

Buttons

When sewing on buttons, use just a few strands of yarn and a smaller needle than the one used for making up. Cut about 12in (30cm) of yarn, then separate about two strands from it. Use these two strands to sew your buttons to the crochet fabric.

Finishing off toys

If your toy is going to be loved and played with daily, you need to make sure the finishing is sturdy. You can use the yarn ends left when you have fastened off each piece (make sure you leave them long). With limbs and body parts, such as for the Panda Comforter, use small neat stitches to attach one part to another.

Using a pompom maker

Pompoms are used to embellish the Pompom Bunting, the Bobble Hat, and the Striped Beret.

1 Open out the two sections on one side of the pompom maker and wrap your yarn tightly around both pieces. Continue until you have filled the whole side.

2 Repeat on the other side.

3 Close both sides to make a complete circle. With sharp, pointed scissors, cut between the ridges around the edge of the circle.

4 Tie 12in (30cm) of your yarn tightly around the middle of the pompom maker in a secure knot.

5 Carefully pull apart the pompom maker from the centre to release the pompom. Trim the pompom with scissors to make sure it looks even and fluffy.

Using a pompom maker

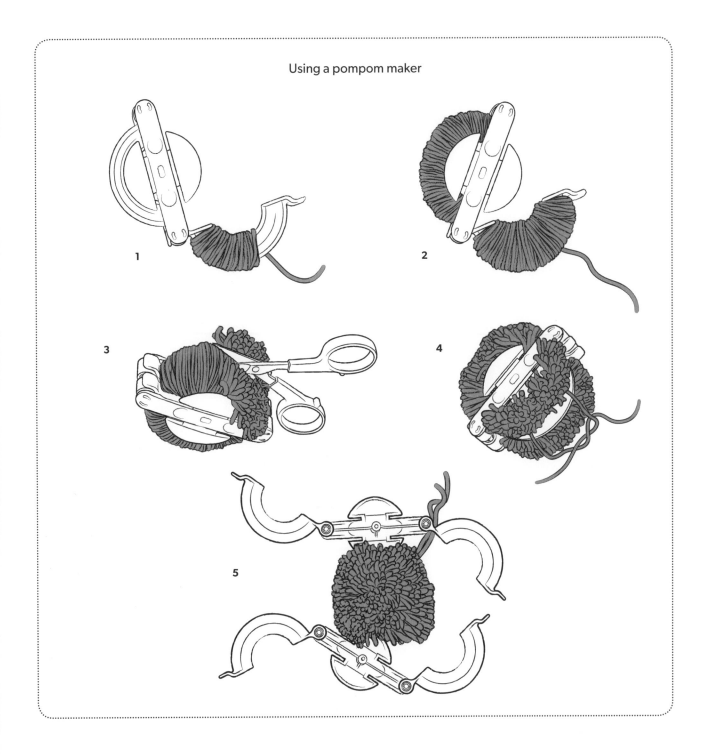

Embroidery stitches

Embroidery techniques are used to give the face of the Panda Comforter extra detail, and for the face of the bears on the Toy Blocks. You will need a tapestry needle and some embroidery thread to sew these stitches on the surface of your piece. If you have never done any embroidery before, try making a small square of double crochet fabric and practise a few techniques first.

Back stitch

Back stitch is excellent for creating a straight line. Using the illustration as a guide, bring your needle up through your fabric at A and then push the needle back down at B. Bring the needle up again at C, and then down again at A. Work along like this to create a neat continuous line.

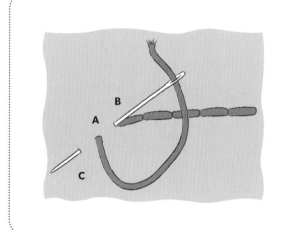

Satin stitch

Satin stitch is used to make a filled-in area, such as the nose of the Panda Comforter or the bear side of the Toy Blocks. Make long stitches next to each other to make the shape you want.

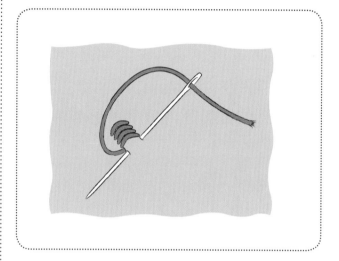

Blocking

One of the most useful techniques you can learn is to 'block' your work into shape once it is finished. Blocking your work can really transform your projects. During the making process, the fibres of the yarn can become crumpled and creased. By blocking your work, the fibres can relax, and the stitches become regular and even.

When you have finished a mountain of squares, the temptation is to start joining your rows as soon as possible. However, if you block each square first, you will find the joining process much simpler, as it is easier to see where the edge stitches correspond for joining the seams together. Block the completed project again once you have finished the edging and woven in all the ends.

Lay out your project on an ironing board or a similar flat and padded surface. Start at one corner and pin gradually along the edges, gently pulling the crochet into place, and secure with a pin. As you work around the edges, you might notice that you have pulled one area more taut than another. Simply remove the pins and reshape. Once you are happy with the overall dimensions, spray the item all over with tepid water. Then leave the crochet to dry completely. Ideally, you should leave your work for two or three days if you can.

Handy tip

If you find that the edges of your blankets go wavy and frilled instead of flat, trying using a hook one size smaller than you used for the squares.

the projects

Cheery Coaster

Crochet is a fabulous technique for making handy coasters.
You can use up any scraps of yarn you have stashed away
and pick out colours to match your decor.

Finished size

4¼in (11cm) in diameter

You will need

- Stylecraft Classique Cotton 4ply 100%cotton (199yd/182m per 50g ball):
  To make the coaster featured at the front of the image, use a small amount of 3672 Poppy (A), 3094 Fondant (B) and 3660 White (C)
- 4mm (UK8:USG/6) crochet hook
- Tapestry needle

Tension

Tension is not essential for this project.

Notes

You can use up any small amounts of yarn to create your own colourways.

Beg puff stitch: 3 ch, *yrh, insert into st, yrh and draw loop through st, drawing loop up to the height of the sts in the row: rep from * three times into the same st, 9 loops on the hook, yrh and draw loop through all loops on hook. (See page 46.)

Puff stitch: *yrh, insert into st, yrh and draw loop through st, drawing loop up to the height of the sts in the row: rep from * three times into the same st, 9 loops on the hook, yrh and draw loop through all loops on hook. Puff completed. (See page 46.)

Crab stitch: Insert hook from front to back in st to the right of the last one, yrh, draw a loop through, yrh and draw through both loops on the hook. (See page 45.)

Coaster

Round 1: Using 4mm hook and A, ch 4 sts, join with a sl st to form a ring.

Round 2: Beg puff, 1 ch, *1 puff in ring, 1 ch; rep from * six times, sl st in top of 3 ch. Fasten off (8 puffs).

Round 3: Attach yarn B in any ch sp, beg puff, 1 puff in same ch sp, *2 puffs in next ch sp; rep from * six times, sl st in top of 3 ch. Fasten off (16 puffs).

Round 4: Attach yarn C in between any 2 puffs, beg puff, 1 puff in same sp, 1 puff in next sp, *2 puffs in between next sp, 1 puff in next sp; rep from * six times, sl st in top of 3 ch. Fasten off (24 puffs).

Round 5: Attach yarn A in between any 2 puffs, beg puff, 1 puff in same sp, 1 puff in next 2 sp, *2 puffs in next sp, 1 puff in next 2 sp; rep from * six times, sl st in top of 3 ch. Fasten off (32 puffs).

Round 6: Attach yarn B in between any 2 puffs, beg puff, 1 puff in same sp, 1 puff in next 3 sp, *2 puffs in next sp, 1 puff in next 3 sp; rep from * six times, sl st in top of 3 ch. Fasten off (40 puffs).

Round 7: Attach yarn A in between any 2 puffs, 1 ch, work in crab stitch around, sl st in ch. Fasten off.

Finishing

Weave in all ends.

Perfect Potholder

Potholders are invaluable in the kitchen. They are useful for lifting saucepan lids to see how your cooking is coming along or protecting a work surface from a hot pan.

Finished size

6 x 6in (15 x 15cm)

You will need

- Paintbox Yarns Cotton Aran, 100% cotton (93yd/85m per 50g ball):
  1 x 50g ball 623 Buttercup Yellow (A)
  1 x 50g ball 605 Stormy Grey (B)
  1 x 50g ball 603 Champagne White (C)
- 5mm (UK6:USH/8) crochet hook
- Tapestry needle

Tension

Tension is not essential for this project.

Potholder sides

(make 2)

Round 1: Using 5mm hook and A, ch 4 sts, join with sl st to form a ring.

Round 2: Ch 1, 8 dc into ring, join with sl st to 1 ch. Break off yarn A.

Round 3: Attach yarn B, 3 ch, 2 tr into same st, 1 ch, *(3 tr, 1 ch) into next st; rep from * six times, join with sl st into third of 3 ch at beg of round (8 tr clusters). Break off yarn B.

Round 4: Attach yarn A in any 1 ch, (1 dc, 3 ch) into same sp, *(1 dc, 3 ch) into next ch sp; rep from * six times, join with sl st to first dc.

Round 5: Attach yarn C in any 3 ch sp with a sl st, 3 ch (counts as first tr) (2 tr, 3 ch, 3 tr) into same ch sp, 1 ch, 3 tr into next 3 ch sp, 1 ch, *(3 tr, 3 ch, 3 tr) into next ch sp, 1 ch, 3 tr into next 3 ch sp, 1 ch; rep from * twice, join with sl st into third of 3 ch at beg of round. Break off yarn C.

Round 6: Attach yarn A in any corner 3 ch sp with a sl st, 1 ch (1 dc, 3 ch, 1 dc) into same sp, 3 ch, (1 dc into next 1 ch sp, 3 ch) twice, *(1 dc, 3 ch, 1 dc) into next 3 ch corner sp, 3 ch, (1 dc into next 1 ch sp, 3 ch) twice; rep from * twice, join with sl st into first dc. Break off yarn A.

Round 7: Attach yarn B to any 3 ch corner sp, 3 ch (counts as 1 tr), (2 tr, 3 ch, 3 tr) into same sp, 1 ch, (3 tr into next 3 ch sp, 1 ch) three times, *(3 tr, 3 ch, 3 tr) into next 3 ch corner sp, 1 ch, (3 tr into next 3 ch sp, 1 ch) three times; rep from * twice, join with sl st into third of 3 ch. Break off yarn B.

Round 8: Attach yarn A in any corner 3 ch sp with a sl st, 1 ch, (1 dc, 3 ch, 1 dc) into same sp, 3 ch, (1 dc into next 1 ch sp, 3 ch) four times, *(1 dc, 3 ch, 1 dc) into next 3 ch corner sp, 3 ch, (1 dc into next 1 ch sp, 3 ch) four times; rep from * twice, join with sl st into first dc. Break off yarn A.

Round 9: Attach yarn C to any 3 ch corner sp, 3 ch (counts as 1 tr), (2 tr, 3 ch, 3 tr) into same sp, 1 ch, (3 tr into next 3 ch sp, 1 ch) five times, *(3 tr, 3 ch, 3 tr) into next 3 ch corner sp, 1 ch, (3 tr, into next 3 ch sp, 1 ch) five times; rep from * twice, join with sl st into third of 3 ch. Break off yarn C.

Round 10: Attach yarn A in any corner 3 ch sp with a sl st, 1 ch, (1 dc, 3 ch, 1 dc) into same sp, 3 ch, (1 dc into next 1 ch sp, 3 ch) six times, *(1 dc, 3 ch, 1 dc) into next 3 ch corner sp, 3 ch, (1 dc into next 1 ch sp, 3 ch) six times; rep from * twice, join with sl st into first dc. Break off yarn A.

Round 11: Attach yarn B to any 3 ch corner sp, 3 ch (counts as 1 tr), (2 tr, 3 ch, 3 tr) into same sp, 1 ch, (3 tr into next 3 ch sp, 1 ch) seven times, *(3 tr, 3 ch, 3 tr) into next 3 ch corner sp, 1 ch, (3 tr into next 3 ch sp, 1 ch) seven times; rep from * twice, join with sl st into third of 3 ch. Break off yarn B. Using a tapestry needle, weave in all ends.

Making up

With wrong sides together and working through both layers, join yarn B in any corner, 1 ch, 3 dc in every corner, 1 dc in every tr along the edge, join with sl st to first dc. 5 ch, sl st in the corner, turn, work 7 dc in ch loop.
Fasten off and weave in ends.

Finishing

Gently block the potholder before use (see page 53).

Flower Headband

You will be surprised how useful this accessory is – it will keep your ears warm but doesn't spoil your hairdo. The joyful flower allows you to practise the same principles used for granny squares.

Finished size

9in (23cm) in diameter and 3in (8cm) deep

You will need

- Stylecraft Jeanie, 60% cotton, 40% acrylic (230yd/210m per 100g ball):
  1 x 100g ball 9351 Delta (A)
  1 x 100g ball 9349 Dixie (B)
- 5mm (UK6:USH/8) crochet hook
- Tapestry needle

Tension

4 dc x 3.5 rows for 1 x 1in (2.5 x 2.5cm) square using 5mm hook.

Headband

Row 1: Using 5mm hook and A, ch 74 sts, 1 dc in second ch from hook, 1 dc in each chain to end, turn (73 sts).

Row 2: Ch 1, 1 dc in first dc, (miss 1 dc, 1 ch, 1 dc into next dc) to end, turn.

Row 3: Change to yarn B, 1 ch, 1 dc in first dc, 1 dc in next ch sp, (1 ch, 1 dc in next ch sp), rep to last dc, turn.

Row 4: Ch 1, 1 dc in first dc, (miss 1 dc, 1 ch, 1 dc into next dc) to end, turn.

Rows 5–6: Change to yarn A, rep rows 3 and 4.

Rows 7–8: Change to yarn B, rep rows 3 and 4.

Rows 9–10: Change to yarn A, rep rows 3 and 4.

Rows 11–12: Change to yarn B, rep rows 3 and 4.

Row 13: Change to yarn A, 1 ch, 1 dc in first dc, 1 dc in next ch sp, (1 ch, 1 dc in next ch sp), rep to last dc, turn.

Row 14: Ch 1, 1 dc in first dc, 1 dc in each ch sp and each dc to end. Fasten off, leaving a long tail of yarn.

Flower

Using yarn A, work 6 ch and join with a sl st to form a ring.

Round 1: Ch 6 (counts as 1 tr and 3 ch), (1 tr into ring, 3 ch) seven times, join with sl st into third of 3 ch (8 spaced tr).

Round 2: Change to yarn B, attach to any 3 ch sp, (1 dc, 2 ch, 3 tr, 2 ch, 1 dc) into same sp, (1 dc, 2 ch, 3 tr, 2 ch, 1 dc into next sp) seven times (8 petals).

Round 3: *Ch 5, working behind the petal miss 1 petal, 1 dc into top of next tr of round 1; rep from * to end.

Round 4: *(1 dc, 2 ch, 5 tr, 2 ch, 1 dc) into next 5 ch loop; rep from * to end.

Fasten off and weave in ends.

Finishing

Weave in all ends and block headband gently (see page 53). Sew together the side seams of the headband. Position the flower and sew securely to the headband.

Pompom Bunting

This fun project is ideal for the nursery, garden, kitchen or anywhere you want to add a pop of colour. Ideally, use wool yarn for fluffy pompoms and fine cotton yarn for the string they sit on.

Finished size

69in (1.75m) length of bunting with 8 triangles and 9 pompoms

You will need

- Stylecraft Classique Cotton 4ply, 100% cotton (199yd/182m per 50g ball):
  1 x 50g ball 3660 White
- Assorted colours of leftover DK yarn
- 4mm (UK8:USG/6) crochet hook
- Pompom maker 2in (5cm) in diameter
- Tapestry needle

Tension

Tension is not essential for this project.

Bunting triangles
(make 8)

Round 1: Using 4mm hook and first colour, ch 4 sts, join with a sl st to form a ring.

Round 2: Ch 3 (this counts as first tr), 3 tr into ring, *3 ch, 4 tr; rep from *, 3 ch, sl st into third ch at beg of round (3 tr clusters). Fasten off. Change to second colour.

Round 3: Attach in any 3 ch sp, 3 ch (counts as 1 tr), (3 tr, 3 ch, 4 tr) into same sp, *1 ch, (4 tr, 3 ch, 4 tr) into next 3 ch sp; rep from * once, 1 ch, join with sl st into third of 3 ch. Fasten off. Change to third colour.

Round 4: Attach yarn in any 3 ch sp, 3 ch (counts as 1 tr), (3 tr, 3 ch, 4 tr) into same sp, *1 ch, 4 tr into 1 ch sp, 1 ch, (4 tr, 3 ch, 4 tr) into next 3 ch sp; rep from * once, 1 ch, 4 tr into 1 ch sp, 1 ch, join with sl st into third of 3 ch. Fasten off.

Bunting string

Using A, ch 6 sts, sl st into first ch to make a loop. Ch until string measures 69in (1.75m), 6 ch, sl st in 6th ch from hook. Fasten off. Make 9 pompoms in assorted colours (see page 50). Position each pompom evenly along the string, approximately 6in (15cm) apart. Attach by sewing the finishing tails of each pompom through a chain stitch. Secure firmly with a knot and cut the ends to match the pompoms. Position your triangles between your pompoms and sew one side of the bunting triangle to the top of the bunting string. Decorate your room or garden with pride.

Chic Cushion

Sometimes it is good to let the texture and the pattern of the yarn do all the talking. Sewn together, this granny square pattern makes a lovely criss-cross design. Although the colours are understated, the central flower of each square gives a lovely pop of colour.

Finished size

16½in (42cm) square

You will need

- Stylecraft Life DK, 75% acrylic, 25% wool (326yd/298m per 100g ball): 1 x 100g ball 2422 Damson (A) 1 x 100g ball 2344 Fuchsia (B)
- 3.5mm (UK9:USE/4) crochet hook
- 1 x 16½in (42cm) square cushion pad
- Tapestry needle

Tension

Each square is approximately 6 x 6in (15 x 15cm) using a 3.5mm hook.

Notes

For instructions on puff stitch, see page 46.
Beginning puff (beg puff) is made from 2 tr sts.
Puff (puff) is made from 3 tr sts.

Square
(make 18)

Using 3.5mm hook and B, ch 6 sts, sl st in first ch to form a loop.

Round 1: Ch 3 (counts as 1 tr), beg puff into ring, 1 ch, (puff into ring, 1 ch) seven times, join with sl st in 3 ch (8 tr puffs).

Round 2: Change to A, attach yarn to any 1 ch sp, 3 ch (counts as 1 tr), (beg puff, 2 ch, puff) into ch sp, * 2 ch, 3 tr into next ch sp, 2 ch (puff, 2 ch, puff) in next ch sp; rep from * twice, 2 ch, 3 tr into next ch sp, 2 ch, sl st in 3 ch.

Round 3: Sl st into next 2 ch sp, 3 ch (counts as 1 tr), (beg puff, 2 ch, puff) into ch sp, * 2 ch, 2 tr into next 2 ch sp, 1 tr into each of next 3 tr, 2 tr into next 2 ch sp, 2 ch (puff, 2 ch, puff) in next ch sp; rep from * twice, 2 ch, 2 tr into next 2 ch sp, 1 tr into each of next 3 tr, 2 tr into next 2 ch sp, 2 ch, sl st in 3 ch.

Round 4: Sl st into next 2 ch sp, 3 ch (counts as 1 tr), (beg puff, 2 ch, puff) into ch sp, * 2 ch, 2 tr into next 2 ch sp, 1 tr into each of next 7 tr, 2 tr into next 2 ch sp, 2 ch (puff, 2 ch, puff) in next ch sp; rep from * twice, 2 ch, 2 tr into next 2 ch sp, 1 tr into each of next 7 tr, 2 tr into next 2 ch sp, 2 ch, sl st in 3 ch.

Round 5: Sl st into next 2 ch sp, 3 ch (counts as 1 tr), (beg puff, 2 ch puff) into ch sp, * 2 ch, 2 tr into next 2 ch sp, 1 tr into each of next 11 tr, 2 tr into next 2 ch sp, 2 ch (puff, 2 ch, puff in next ch sp; rep from * twice, 2 ch, 2 tr into next 2 ch sp, 1 tr into each of next 11 tr, 2 tr into next 2 ch sp, 2 ch, sl st in 3 ch.
Fasten off and weave in ends.
Complete 18 squares.

Finishing

Using the photograph as a guide, join the squares together using yarn A, in three rows of three squares. Attach by using sl st in the back loop of each st in each square. Attach both sides of the cushion cover together: work a dc stitch through both sides of the cover in the top of each tr st. Work around three sides, then insert the cushion pad. Crochet the final seam together.

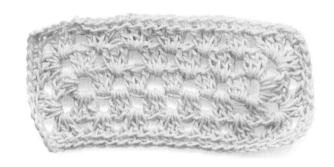

Stylish Tablemat

This chic and simple tablemat makes a perfect housewarming gift. The mat is double-sided, with a rectangular granny-square design on one side and rows of double crochet on the other.

Finished size

12 x 9in (30 x 23cm)

You will need

- Stylecraft Classique Cotton 4ply, 100% cotton (199yd/182m per 50g ball):
  2 x 50g balls 3665 Ivory
- 3mm (UK11:US–) crochet hook

Tension

Granny rectangle: 7 treble clusters x 12 rows for 4 x 4in (10 x 10 cm) square using 3mm hook.

Double crochet: 22 sts x 30 rows for 4 x 4in (10 x 10 cm) square using 3mm hook.

Front

Round 1: Using 3mm hook, ch 21 sts, 3 tr in sixth ch from hook, miss 2 ch, *3 tr in next ch, miss 2 ch; rep from * four times more, 1 tr in last ch.

Round 2: Ch 3 (this counts as first tr), 2 tr, ch 3, 3 tr, ch 3, 3 tr in sp created by last tr of previous round (two corners made), (3 tr in next 2 ch sp) four times, (3 tr, ch 3, 3 tr, ch 3, 3 tr) in 5 ch sp (two corners made), 3 tr in each of next 4 sp between 3 tr clusters of the previous round, sl st into third ch at beg of round. Do not fasten off.

Round 3: Ch 3 (counts as 1 tr), *(3 tr, 3 ch, 3 tr) into next 3 ch sp; rep from *, 3 tr in each of next 5 sp between 3 tr clusters of previous round, ** (3 tr, 3 ch, 3 tr) into next 3 ch sp; rep from **, 3 tr in each of next 4 sp between 3 tr clusters of previous round, 2 tr in next sp, join with sl st into third of 3 ch.

Round 4: Ch 3 (this counts as first tr), 2 tr into same sp, (3 tr, ch 3, 3 tr) into next 3 ch sp, 3 tr into next sp, (3 tr, ch 3, 3 tr) into next 3 ch sp, 3 tr in each of next 6 sp between 3 tr clusters of previous round, (3 tr, ch 3, 3 tr) into next 3 ch sp, 3 tr, (3 tr, ch 3, 3 tr) into next 3 ch sp, 3 tr in each of next 5 sp between 3 tr clusters of previous round, sl st into third ch at beg of round.

Continue to work in rounds, expanding the number of tr clusters until you have worked 14 rounds (62 tr clusters).

Rounds 15–17: Ch 1, work 1 dc tbl into top of every st, work (1 dc tbl, 1 ch, 1 dc tbl) in every corner sp, join with sl st into 1 ch. Fasten off.

Back

Row 1: Using 3mm hook, ch 70 sts, 1 dc in 2nd ch from hook, 1 dc in each ch to end, turn (69 sts).

Row 2: Ch 1, 1 dc in each st to end. Rep row 2 until you have worked 66 rows.

Finishing

Weave in all ends and gently block the blanket. Attach the front and back together by working through both sides with 1 dc in each st and (1 dc, 1 ch 1 dc) in each corner.

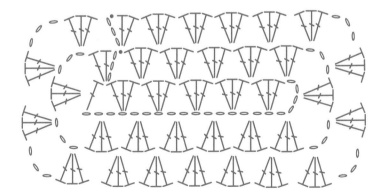

Glasses Case

This is one of the simplest and most useful items to crochet. Make the case in bright colours, and your glasses will never get lost at the bottom of a cavernous bag again.

Finished size

8in (20cm) tall and 3½in (9cm) wide

You will need

- Debbie Bliss Rialto DK, 100% merino wool (115yd/105m per 50g ball):
  1 x 50g ball 33 Charcoal (A)
  1 x 50g ball 69 Citrus (B)
  1 x 50g ball 09 Apple (C)
  1 x 50g ball 75 Petunia (D)
  1 x 50g ball 62 Mulberry (E)
- 4mm (UK8:USG/6) crochet hook
- 1 x ⅝in (15mm) button
- Tapestry needle

Tension

Tension is not essential for this project, but each square is approximately 2¾ x 2¾in (7 x 7cm) using a 4mm hook.

Granny square

Work 9 squares in different colours for rounds 1 and 2, but always work round 3 in yarn A.
Using 4mm hook and B, ch 4 sts, sl st in first ch to form a loop.
Round 1: 3 ch, 2 tr in loop, 3 ch, (3 tr, 3 ch), rep twice more, sl st in 3 ch (4 tr clusters).
Round 2: Change to C, attach yarn to any 3 ch sp, (3 ch, 2 tr, 3 ch, 3 tr, 1 ch) in ch sp, (3 tr, 3 ch, 3 tr, 1 ch) in next ch sp three times, sl st in 3 ch (8 tr clusters).
Round 3: Change to A, attach yarn to any 3 ch sp, (3 ch, 2 tr, 3 ch, 3 tr, 1 ch) in ch sp, (3 tr, 1 ch) in next ch sp, *(3 tr, 3 ch, 3 tr, 1 ch) in next 3 ch sp, (3 tr, 1 ch) in next ch sp; rep from * twice more, sl st in 3 ch (12 tr clusters).
Fasten off.

Finishing

Weave in ends and block each of the squares. Using the diagram as a guide, join the squares together using yarn A. With RS together, whip stitch the seams together (see page 48) through the back loop of each square. You will have two pointed corners at the top of the case. Fold one inside the other. Sew a button at the base of the corner of this square. Then fold over the other square and use the corner of this square as a button loop to close the case.

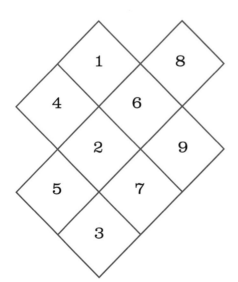

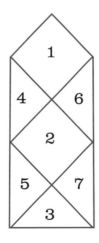

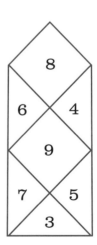

Smart Doorstop

This design makes a pretty yet practical accessory for
a living room or a bedroom. Filled with rice to give it stability,
it will ensure your door stays just where you want it.

Finished size

5in (12.5cm) in diameter and 5½in (14cm) tall

You will need

- Stylecraft Life DK, 75% acrylic, 25% wool, (326yd/298m per 100g ball):
  1 x 100g ball 2422 Damson (A)
  1 x 100g ball 2344 Fuchsia (B)
  1 x 100g ball 2319 Cranberry (C)
- 3.5mm (UK9:USE/4) crochet hook
- 2.2lb (1kg) bag of rice
- A dark opaque stocking or pop sock
- Tapestry needle

Tension

This is not essential, but each square is approximately 6 x 6in (15 x 15cm) using a 3.5mm hook.

Notes

For instructions on puff stitch, see page 46.
Beginning puff (beg puff) is made from 2 tr sts.
Puff (puff) is made from 3 tr sts.

Square

(make 3)

Using 3.5mm hook and B, ch 6 sts, sl st in first ch to form a loop.

Round 1: Ch 3 (counts as 1 tr), beg puff into ring, 1 ch, (puff into ring, 1 ch) seven times, join with sl st in 3 ch (8 tr puffs).

Round 2: Attach yarn A in any 1 ch sp with a sl st, 3 ch (counts as first tr) (2 tr, 3 ch, 3 tr) into same ch sp, 1 ch, 3 tr into next ch sp, 1 ch, *(3 tr, 3 ch, 3 tr) into next ch sp, 1 ch, 3 tr into next ch sp, 1 ch; rep from * twice, join with sl st into third of 3 ch at beg of round. Break off yarn A.

Round 3: Attach yarn B in any corner 3 ch sp with a sl st, 1 ch (1 dc, 3 ch, 1 dc) into same sp, 3 ch, (1 dc into next 1 ch sp, 3 ch) twice, * (1 dc, 3 ch, 1 dc) into next 3 ch corner sp, 3 ch, (1 dc into next 1 ch sp, 3 ch) twice; rep from * twice, join with sl st into first dc. Break off yarn B.

Round 4: Attach yarn C to any 3 ch corner sp, 3 ch (counts as 1 tr), (2 tr, 3 ch, 3 tr) into same sp, 1 ch, (3 tr into next 3 ch sp, 1 ch) three times, * (3 tr, 3 ch, 3 tr) into next 3 ch corner sp, 1 ch, (3 tr into next 3 ch sp, 1 ch) three times; rep from * twice, join with sl st into third of 3 ch. Break off yarn C.

Round 5: Attach yarn B in any corner 3 ch sp with a sl st, 1 ch (1 dc, 3 ch, 1 dc) into same sp, 3 ch, (1 dc into next 1 ch sp, 3 ch) four times, * (1 dc, 3 ch, 1 dc) into next 3 ch corner sp, 3 ch, (1 dc into next 1 ch sp, 3 ch) four times; rep from * twice, join with sl st into first dc. Break off yarn B.

Round 6: Attach yarn A to any 3 ch corner sp, 3 ch (counts as 1 tr), (2 tr, 3 ch, 3 tr) into same sp, 1 ch, (3 tr into next 3 ch sp, 1 ch) five times, * (3 tr, 3 ch, 3 tr) into next 3 ch corner sp, 1 ch, (3 tr, into next 3 ch sp, 1 ch) five times; rep from * twice, join with sl st into third of 3 ch.
Fasten off and weave in ends.

Top

Using 3.5mm hook and B, ch 6 sts, sl st in first ch to form a loop.

Round 1: Ch 3 (counts as 1 tr), beg puff into ring, 1 ch, (puff into ring, 1 ch) seven times, join with sl st in 3 ch (8 tr puffs).

Round 2: Attach yarn A in any ch sp, 3 ch, beg puff, 1 puff in same ch sp, *2 puff in next ch sp; rep from * six times, sl st in top of 3 ch (16 puffs).

Round 3: Sl st into next sp between puffs, 3 ch, beg puff, 1 puff between each two puff of previous round, sl st in top of 3 ch (16 puffs).

Round 4: Sl st into next sp between puffs, 3 ch, beg puff, 1 puff in same sp, 1 puff in next sp, *2 puff in next sp, 1 puff in next sp; rep from * six times, sl st in top of 3 ch. Fasten off (24 puffs).

Base

Using 3.5mm hook and A, make a magic ring.

Round 1: 1 ch, 8 dc into centre of ring.

Round 2: 2 dc into each st (16 sts).

Round 3: (1 dc, dc2inc) eight times (24 sts).

Round 4: Work 1 round straight (24 sts).

Round 5: (2 dc, dc2inc) eight times (32 sts).

Round 6: Work 1 round straight (32 sts).

Round 7: (3 dc, dc2inc) eight times (40 sts).

Round 8: (4 dc, dc2inc) eight times (48 sts).

Round 9: Work 1 round straight (48 sts).

Round 10: (5 dc, dc2inc) eight times (56 sts).

Round 11: (6 dc, dc2inc) eight times (64 sts).

Round 12: Work 1 round straight (64 sts).

Round 13: (7 dc, dc2inc) eight times (72 sts).

Round 14: (8 dc, dc2inc) eight times (80 sts).

Round 15: Work 1 round straight (80 sts).

Fasten off and weave in ends.

Finishing

Make the sides of the doorstop by attaching the side edges of the squares together to form a cylinder. With RS together and using B, attach yarn in a 3 ch corner sp, 1 dc, in ch sp, *3 ch, 1 dc in next ch sp; rep six times. With RS together, attach the top by joining yarn A to any ch sp and sp between puffs, * 3 ch, 1 dc, rep around easing the top of the doorstop into the top of the squares. Turn the crochet out so that it is the right side out. Place the bag of rice in a dark opaque stocking or sock and sew the end together. Place this inside the crochet cover. Place the base onto the bottom of the crochet cover. Using yarn A, dc the edge of the base and the bottom of the granny square cylinder together. Fasten off and weave in ends.

Snug Cowl

There is something very comforting about a soft cowl to keep your neck warm. The subtle tones of this cowl are worked in granny stripes as a large loop with a pretty shell edging.

Finished size

25¼in (64cm) in circumference and
7½in (19cm) deep

You will need

- Debbie Bliss Baby Cashmerino,
  55% wool, 33% acrylic, 12%
  cashmere (137yd/125m per
  50g ball):
  1 x ball 012 Silver (A)
  1 x ball 026 Duck Egg (B)
  1 x ball 086 Coral (C)
  1 x ball 101 Ecru (D)
  1 x ball 018 Citrus (E)
  1 x ball 001 Primrose (F)
- 3.5mm (UK9:USE/4) crochet hook
- 4mm (UK8:USG/6) crochet hook
- Tapestry needle

Tension

Tension is not essential for
this project.

Cowl

Using 4mm hook and A, ch 102 sts,
join with a sl st to form a loop.

Round 1: 1 ch, 1 dc in ch at base of
hook, dc into each ch to end, join
with a sl st to first ch. Fasten off
(102 sts).

Round 2: Using 3.5mm hook, attach
B to any dc, 3 ch (counts as first tr),
2 tr into same dc, *miss 2 dc, 1 ch,
3 tr into next dc; rep from * around,
miss 2 dc, 1 ch, sl st into third of 3
ch at beg of round. Fasten off
(34 tr clusters).

Round 3: Attach C in any ch sp with
a sl st, 3 ch (counts as first tr), 2 tr into
same ch sp, *1 ch, miss 3 tr, 3 tr into
next ch sp; rep from * around, 1 ch,
miss 3 tr, sl st into third of 3 ch at beg
of round. Fasten off.

Round 3 forms the pattern. Continue
working in this manner using the
colour sequence B, C, D, E, F
until you have worked the colour
sequence three times. Work a
further 1 round using B.

Round 18: Attach A to any tr, 1 ch,
1 dc at base of ch, work 1 dc into
every tr, miss every ch sp, join with a
sl st to first ch (102 sts).

Round 19: 1 ch, dc into each st
around, join with a sl st to first ch.

Round 20: *Miss 2 dc, 5 tr in
next dc, miss 2 dc, sl st in next
dc; rep from * around. Fasten off
(17 shell clusters).

Finishing

Using 3.5mm hook, add a shell
edging to the base of your cowl
along the bottom edge to complete
it. Turn your work around so that the
beginning chain is uppermost.
Attach A to any ch, *miss 2 ch, 5 tr
in next ch, miss 2 ch, sl st in next
ch; rep from * around. Fasten off
(17 shell clusters).

Weave in all ends.

Draught Excluder

This draught excluder is a wonderfully practical way to keep the cold of winter at bay. The design uses the treble clusters that are part of the classic granny-square style but made up in smart stripes.

Finished size

34 x 8in (86 x 20cm)

You will need

- Stylecraft Life DK, 75% acrylic, 25% wool (326yd/298m per 100g ball):
  1 x 100g ball 2309 Heather (A)
  1 x 100g ball 2301 Rose (B)
  1 x 100g ball 2319 Cranberry (C)
- 4mm (UK8:USG/6) crochet hook
- Tapestry needle
- Standard draught excluder cushion pad, 34 x 8in (86 x 20cm)

Tension

6 treble clusters x 8 rows for 4 x 4in (10 x 10 cm) square using 4mm hook.

Draught excluder

Row 1: Using 4mm hook and A, ch 80 sts, 1 dc in 2nd ch from hook, 1 dc in each chain to end, turn (79 sts).

Row 2: Ch 3 (this counts as first tr), 1 tr into same place, (miss 2 dc, 3 tr into next dc), rep to last 3 sts, miss 2 dc, 2 tr into last dc, turn (27 tr clusters).

Row 3: Ch 3 (counts as 1 tr), *(3 tr into next sp between tr groups) to end, 1 tr into third of 3 ch, turn (26 tr clusters).

Rep rows 2 and 3 using yarn B, then follow with two rows in yarn C.

Rep the pattern using the colour sequence 2 rows in A, 2 rows in B and 2 rows in C, 12 times. Work a further 2 rows in A.

Next row: Ch 1, 1 dc in each tr to end. Fasten off.

Finishing

Weave in all ends and gently block the draught excluder. Wrap the crochet fabric around the cushion pad. Attach the seams together by working through both sides with 1 dc in each st and (1 dc, 1 ch 1 dc) in each corner. Weave in ends.

Lazy-edged Blanket

Everyone loves traditional vintage-style granny-square blankets but they take ages to make. So if you are short of time this pattern is the perfect shortcut. Choose an open-weave or fleece blanket, then add a granny-style edging for a unique crafty finish.

Finished size

The edging is about 1¼in (3cm) deep

You will need

- Stylecraft Life DK, 75% premium acrylic, 25% wool (326yd/298m per 100g ball):
  1 x 100g ball 2341 Silver Grey
- 2.5mm (UK12:USC2) crochet hook
- 3.5mm (UK9:USE/4) crochet hook
- Tapestry needle
- Blanket, 48 x 72in (120 x 180cm)

Tension

Tension is not essential to this project.

Notes

Spike stitch: Work to where the spike stitch is required. Push the hook through the fabric to the reverse of the work. Wrap the yarn round the hook, then draw through to the front of the work to form another loop on the hook. Do not pull the yarn too tight, as this will make the fabric pucker. Wrap the yarn round the hook and complete the stitch.

Edging

If you have an open-weave blanket, use your crochet hook to create the foundation stitch around the edge of the blanket in spike stitch. Some fleece blankets have a blanket stitch edging already, so you can use that as your foundation row. If the weave of the blanket is impenetrable, use blanket stitch (see page 47) for the base of the crochet stitches. Make sure each stitch is evenly spaced, about ½in (1.25cm) apart.

Foundation row: Insert the 2.5mm hook from the front to the back of the blanket about ½in (1.25cm) from the edge, hook the yarn over, then pull it to the right side, yo and pull through to create a spike st, 3 ch, (1 spike st, 3 ch), rep around the edge keeping the spike sts evenly spaced about ½in (1.25cm) apart, sl st to join to the top of the first spike st. Do not fasten off.

Row 2: Change to 3.5mm hook, 3 ch (counts as 1 tr), 1 tr in each ch around and work (1 tr, 3 ch, 1 tr) in each corner ch, join with a sl st to 3 ch.

Row 3: *Ch 3, miss 2 tr, sl st in next tr; rep from * around and work (1 sl st, 3 ch, 1 sl st) into every 3 ch corner, join with sl st in the beg st.

Row 4: Sl st to first 3 ch, 3 ch (counts as 1 htr and 1 ch), *1 htr in next 3 ch sp, 1 ch; rep from * around and work (1 htr, 1 ch, 1 htr, 1 ch, 1 htr, 1 ch) into each 3 ch corner sp, join with sl st in first 3 ch.

Row 5: Sl st to the next ch sp, *3 ch, sl st in centre of next 3 ch sp; rep around and work (1 sl st, 3 ch, 1 sl st) into every 3 ch corner, join with sl st in the beg st.

Fasten off securely and weave in ends.

Rainbow Rattle

This is a pretty and thoughtful gift to make for a new baby. Made in bright colours, this granny square rattle will certainly grab their attention.

Finished size

7½in (19cm) tall and 3½cm (9cm) wide

You will need

- Stylecraft Classique Cotton 4ply, 100% cotton (199yd/182m per 50g ball):
  1 x 50g ball 3672 Poppy (A)
  1 x 50g ball 3662 Sunflower (B)
  1 x 50g ball 3663 Soft Lime (C)
  1 x 50g ball 3667 Sky Blue (D)
  1 x 50g ball 3095 Greek Blue (E)
  1 x 50g ball 3660 White (F)
- 3mm (UK11:US–) crochet hook
- Polyester stuffing
- 6in (15cm) lolly stick
- Piece of white felt, large enough to cut out two squares 2½ x 2½in (6.5 x 6.5cm)
- Small bell
- Tapestry needle

Tension

Tension is not essential for this project, but each square is approximately 3¼ x 3¼in (8 x 8cm) using a 3mm hook.

Note

The handle is worked in spirals using the magic ring technique (see page 44). The granny square is made in a round and sewn to the top of the handle.

Granny square
(make 2)

Using 3mm hook and A, ch 4 sts, sl st in first ch to form a loop.

Round 1: 3 ch, 2 tr in loop, 3 ch, (3 tr, 3 ch), rep twice more, sl st in 3 ch (4 tr clusters).

Round 2: Change to B, attach yarn to any 3 ch sp, (3 ch, 2 tr, 3 ch, 3 tr, 1 ch) in ch sp, (3 tr, 3 ch, 3 tr, 1 ch) in next ch sp three times, sl st in 3 ch (8 tr clusters).

Round 3: Change to C, attach yarn to any 3 ch sp, (3 ch, 2 tr, 3 ch, 3 tr, 1 ch) in ch sp, (3 tr, 1 ch) in next ch sp, *(3 tr, 3 ch, 3 tr, 1 ch) in next 3 ch sp, (3 tr, 1 ch) in next ch sp; rep from * twice more, sl st in 3 ch (12 tr clusters).

Round 4: Change to D, attach yarn to any 3 ch sp, 2 ch, 1 dc in ch sp, 1 dc in the top of every tr and every 1 ch sp, work (1 dc, 1 ch, 1 dc) into every 3 ch corner sp, join with sl st to first ch.

Round 5: Change to E, attach yarn to any 1 ch sp, 2 ch, 1 dc in ch sp, 1 dc in the top of every dc, work (1 dc, 1 ch, 1 dc) into every 1 ch corner sp, join with sl st to first ch.

Fasten off and weave in ends.

Handle

Using 3mm hook and F, make a magic ring (see page 44).

Round 1: 1 ch, 6 dc into the centre of the ring.

Round 2: 2 dc into each st (12 sts).

Round 3: (1 dc, dc2inc) six times (18 sts).

Round 4: Work 1 round straight.

Rounds 5–6: Change to A, work 2 rounds straight.

Rounds 7–8: Change to F, work 2 rounds straight.

Rounds 9–10: Change to B, work 2 rounds straight.

Rounds 11–12: Change to F, work 2 rounds straight.

Rounds 13–14: Change to C, work 2 rounds straight.

Rounds 15–16: Change to F, work 2 rounds straight.

Rounds 17–18: Change to D, work 2 rounds straight.

Rounds 19–20: Change to F, work 2 rounds straight.

Rounds 21–22: Change to E, work 2 rounds straight.

Rounds 23–25: Change to F, work 3 rounds straight.

Round 26: (1 dc, dc2tog) six times (12 sts).

Round 27: Work 1 round straight. Fasten off.

Finishing

Weave in ends and block each of the squares. Cut out two pieces of felt, each measuring 2½ x 2½in (6.5 x 6.5cm). Place the pieces together and sew around all four sides, keeping one corner open. Place the bell inside the felt pillow and stuff with a small amount of stuffing. Place the front and back of the granny squares WS together. Using E, attach yarn 4 sts from one corner, 1 ch, 1 dc in both sides of the granny square and work (1 dc, 1 ch, 1 dc) in each corner space. Fasten off when you are four stitches from the last corner. Carefully place the stuffed pillow inside the granny square pillow. Ease the corners of the pillow into the corners of the granny squares. Begin to stuff the handle of the rattle. Then place the lolly stick down the centre of the handle. Work additional stuffing around the stick and make sure the handle is firm. Place the granny square pillow on top of the stick and pull the open edge over the top of the handle. Sew firmly in place.

Bolster Cushion

You will be surprised how quickly you can make this pretty cushion cover. This pattern uses the traditional granny square, but you join the squares as you go. Making the cover in one colour creates the appearance of a lovely lacy pattern.

Finished size

17in (43cm) long and 20in (51cm) in circumference

You will need

- Stylecraft Batik DK, 80% premium acrylic, 20% wool (151yd/138m per 50g ball):
  3 x 50g balls 1916 Rose
- 3.5mm (UK9:USE/4) crochet hook
- 17in (43cm) long and 20in (51cm) circumference bolster cushion pad
- 2 x ¾in (20mm) buttons
- Tapestry needle
- Sewing needle and thread

Tension

Tension is not essential for this project, but each square is approximately 2¼ x 2¼in (6 x 6cm) using a 3.5mm hook.

Note

The main part of the cushion cover is made up of 8 rows of 8 granny squares – 64 granny squares in total. For this pattern, I would suggest joining the squares as you make them (see page 49). However, if you prefer, you can make all 36 and join them at the end with a whip stitch (see page 48) through the back loop of the last row of each square.

Granny square
(make 64)

Using 3.5mm hook, ch 4 sts, sl st in first ch to form a loop.

Round 1: 3 ch, 2 tr in loop, 3 ch, (3 tr, 3 ch), rep twice more, sl st in 3 ch (4 tr clusters).

Round 2: Sl st to next 3 ch sp, (3 ch, 2 tr, 3 tr, 3 tr, 1 ch) in ch sp, (3 tr, 3 ch, 3 tr, 1 ch) in next ch sp three times, sl st in 3 ch (8 tr clusters). Fasten off.

Join as you go motif

Work round 1 of standalone square motif. Line up the square in progress to the square you need to attach.

Round 2: Sl st to next 3 ch sp, (3 ch, 2 tr, 1 ch, 1 sl st in corner 3 ch sp of opposite square, 1 ch, 3 tr back in ch sp of working square, 1 sl st in 1 ch sp of opposite square), *(3 tr in next 3 ch sp of working square, 1 ch, 1 sl st in corner 3 ch sp of opposite square, 1 ch, 3 tr back in ch sp of working square, 1 sl st in 1 ch sp of opposite square); rep from * if additional side needs to be joined; if no joining is needed, cont around as for stand-alone square.

Continue in this way, joining the working motif to an adjacent motif if needed or working as for standalone square if no join is necessary.

Bolster ends

Using 3.5mm hook, ch 4 sts, sl st in first ch to form a loop.

Round 1: Ch 3 (counts as 1 tr), 1 ch, (1 tr, 1 ch into loop) seven times, join with sl st in 3 ch (8 tr).

Round 2: Ch 3, 1 tr, 1 ch into same sp at base of 3 ch, (2 tr, 1 ch in next ch sp) seven times, join with sl st in 3 ch (8 x 2 tr clusters).

Round 3: Ch 3, 2 tr, 2 ch into same sp at base of 3 ch, (3 tr, 2 ch in next ch sp) seven times, join with sl st in 3 ch (8 x 3 tr clusters).

Round 4: Ch 3, 1 tr, 1 ch, 2 tr into same sp at base of 3 ch, *(2 tr, 1 ch) twice in next 2 ch sp, rep seven times, join with sl st in 3 ch (16 x 2 tr clusters).

Round 5: Ch 3, 1 tr, 2 ch into same sp at base of 3 ch, (2 tr, 2 ch in next ch sp) fifteen times, join with sl st in 3 ch (16 x 2 tr clusters).

Round 6: Ch 3, 2 tr, 2 ch into same sp at base of 3 ch, (3 tr, 2 ch in next ch sp) fifteen times, join with sl st in 3 ch (16 x 3 tr clusters).

Finishing

Weave in ends. Pull the main part of the bolster cushion cover over the cushion. Then, using a slip stitch, sew the last round of each end to the ends of the granny squares. Fasten a shell button in the centre of each end for extra detail.

Chunky Lap Blanket

This is the perfect weekend project: it is quick and easy to make, and you can snuggle up on the sofa while you are making it. The single-colour design and chunky yarn give this project a chic look.

Finished size
39in (100cm) square

You will need
- Stylecraft Weekender Super Chunky, 100% acrylic (109yd/100m per 100g ball): 4 x 100g balls 3684 Indigo
- 9mm (UK00:USM/13) crochet hook
- Tapestry needle

Tension
2.5 treble clusters x 3.5 rows for 4 x 4in (10 x 10cm) square.

Blanket
Round 1: Using 9mm hook, ch 10 sts, join with a sl st to form a ring.

Round 2: Ch 3 (this counts as first tr), 23 tr into ring, sl st into third ch at beg of round (24 tr).

Round 3: 5 ch (counts as 1 tr and 2 ch), (miss 1 st of previous round, 1 tr, 2 ch), rep around, join with a sl st into third of 5 ch (12 tr spaces).

Round 4: Sl st into next 2 ch sp, 3 ch (counts as 1 tr), 3 tr into same sp, 2 ch, (4 tr, 2 ch) into each ch sp to end, join with a sl st into third of 3 ch.

Round 5: Sl st into next 2 ch sp, * (2 htr, 1 tr, 1 dtr, 2 ch, 1 dtr, 1 tr, 2 htr) into same 2 ch sp, 1 sl st into centre of 4 tr group; rep from * around, join with a sl st into first htr (12 petals). Fasten off.

Round 6: Join with a sl st to the top of one petal in 2 ch sp, ch 4, sl st in next 2 ch sp, 4 ch, sl st in next 2 ch sp, * 4 ch, 1 dtr in sl st between two petals, (4 ch, sl st in next 2 ch sp) three times; rep from * twice, 4 ch, 1 dtr in sl st between two petals, 4 ch, sl st in first 2 ch sp.

Round 7: (Ch 3 (counts as 1 tr), 2 tr, 1 ch, 3 tr, 1 ch) in 4 ch sp, (3 tr, 1 ch, 3 tr, 1 ch in next ch sp) twice, * 3 ch, (3 tr, 1 ch, 3tr, 1 ch in next ch sp) four times; rep from * twice more, 3 ch, (3 tr, 1 ch, 3 tr, 1 ch in next ch sp), sl st in 3 ch (32 tr clusters). Fasten off.

Round 8: Attach yarn to any 3 ch sp, (3 ch, 2 tr, 3 ch, 3 tr, 1 ch) in ch sp, (3 tr, 1 ch in next ch sp) seven times, *(3 tr, 3 ch, 3 tr, 1 ch) in next 3 ch sp, (3 tr, 1 ch in next ch sp) seven times; rep from * twice more, sl st in 3 ch (36 tr clusters).

Continue increasing the granny square in this manner until you have 80 treble clusters.

Rounds 20–23: Ch 1, work 1 dc tbl into the top of every st and ch sp, work (1 dc tbl, 1 ch, 1 dc tbl) in every corner sp, join with a sl st into 1 ch. Fasten off.

Finishing
Weave in all ends and gently block blanket (see page 53).

Bobble Hat

This pretty hat uses granny squares to create its cosy warmth.
I used subtle pastel shades, but you could make more of a
statement by using a dark background and clashing neon colours.

Finished size

21¼in (54cm) in circumference and 8¾in (22cm) deep

You will need

• Debbie Bliss Baby Cashmerino, 55% wool, 33% acrylic, 12% cashmere (137yd/125m per 50g ball):
  1 x 50g ball 012 Silver (A)
  1 x 50g ball 026 Duck Egg (B)
  1 x 50g ball 086 Coral (C)
  1 x 50g ball 101 Ecru (D)
  1 x 50g ball 018 Citrus (E)
  1 x 50g ball 001 Primrose (F)
• 3.5mm (UK9:USE/4) crochet hook
• Tapestry needle
• Pompom maker 3⅜in (8.5cm) in diameter

Tension

Tension is not essential for this project, but each square motif is approximately 4 x 4in (10 x 10cm).

Note

You will need to make ten square motifs for this design. You will arrange two rows of five squares. I would suggest you make five single-colour squares and five multicoloured squares. However, ensure that Round 6 is always completed in Silver (A).

Multicoloured square (make 5)

Round 1: Using 3.5mm hook and F, ch 4 sts, join with a sl st to form a ring.

Round 2: Ch 3 (this counts as first tr), 11 tr into ring, sl st into third ch at beg of round (12 sts). Fasten off.

Round 3: Attach yarn D between any two tr sts, 3 ch (counts as 1 tr), 1 tr into same sp, *2 tr between next 2 sts; rep from * to end, join with a sl st into third of 3 ch. Fasten off. Change to any yarn colour (not A) (24 sts).

Round 4: Attach yarn in between any 2 tr groups, 3 ch (counts as first tr), 2 tr into same sp, *3 tr between next 2 tr groups; rep from * to end, join with a sl st into third of 3 ch. Fasten off (12 tr clusters).

Round 5: Attach yarn A in between any 3 tr groups, 3 ch (counts as first tr) (2 tr, 3 ch, 3 tr) into sp, *1 ch (3 htr, 1 ch in sp between next two 3 tr groups) twice, (3 tr, 3 ch, 3 tr) between next two 3 tr groups; rep from * twice, 1 ch (3 htr, 1 ch in sp between next two 3 tr groups) twice, join with a sl st into third of 3 ch (16 tr clusters).

Round 6: Sl st across 2 sts to corner ch sp, 3 ch (counts as first tr), (2 tr, 3 ch, 3 tr) into sp, *(1 ch, 3 tr into next ch sp) three times, 1 ch, (3 tr, 3 ch, 3 tr) into next ch sp; rep from * twice, (1 ch, 3 tr into next ch sp) three times, 1 ch, sl st into third of 3 ch at beg of round. Fasten off (20 tr clusters).

Single-coloured square (make 5)

Round 1: Using 3.5mm hook and any yarn (not A or D), ch 4 sts, join with a sl st to form a ring.

Round 2: Ch 3 (this counts as first tr), 11 tr into ring, sl st into third ch at beg of round (12 sts).

Round 3: 3 ch (counts as 1 tr), 1 tr into same sp, *2 tr between next 2 sts; rep from * to end, join with a sl st into third of 3 ch (24 sts)

Round 4: 3 ch (counts as first tr), 2 tr at base of ch, *3 tr between next 2 tr groups; rep from * to end, join with a sl st into third of 3 ch (12 tr clusters).

Round 5: Sl st across 3 sts and into gap between next two 3 tr groups, 3 ch (counts as first tr) (2 tr, 3 ch, 3 tr) into sp, *1 ch (3 htr, 1 ch in sp between next two 3 tr groups) twice, (3 tr, 3 ch, 3 tr) between next two 3 tr groups; rep from * twice, 1 ch (3 htr, 1 ch in sp between next two 3 tr groups) twice, join with a sl st into third of 3 ch. Fasten off (16 tr clusters).

Round 6: Attach A to any corner ch sp, 3 ch (counts as first tr), (2 tr, 3 ch, 3 tr) into sp, *(1 ch, 3 tr into next ch sp) three times, 1 ch, (3 tr, 3 ch, 3 tr) into next ch sp; rep from * twice, (1 ch, 3 tr into next ch sp) three times, 1 ch, sl st into third of 3 ch at beg of round. Fasten off (20 tr clusters).

Making up

Using 3.5mm hook and A, sl st two rows of five motifs together. Sl st the edges together to form a circle.

Hat band

Round 1: Using 3.5mm hook and A, attach yarn to any st on the edge with a sl st, 1 ch, 1 dc in each dc, ch and seam around, sl st into ch.

Rounds 2–4: 1 ch, 1 dc in each dc, sl st into ch. Fasten off. Change to C.

Round 5: 1 ch, 1 dc in each dc, sl st into ch. Fasten off.

Finishing

Weave in all ends. Using A, sew a running stitch along the top seams of the hat and gather together. Sew the gather firmly. Make a pompom using C and sew securely to the top of the hat.

Panda Comforter

For young babies, this cute comforter or lovey makes
the perfect cuddly companion to snuggle up
with in their cot or pram at nap time.

Finished size

Panda head approximately 2in (5cm) tall and 3in (8cm) wide
Blanket approximately 10¼in (26cm) wide

You will need

- Debbie Bliss Baby Cashmerino, 55% wool, 33% acrylic, 12% cashmere (137yd/125m per 50g ball):
  1 x 50g ball 300 Black (A)
  1 x 50g ball 101 Ecru (B)
- 3.5mm (UK9:USE/4) crochet hook
- Tapestry needle
- Polyester stuffing
- Safety eyes

Tension

Tension is not essential for this project.

Note

The panda head, arms and ears are worked in spirals using the magic ring technique (see page 44). The granny square blanket is made in a round and sewn to the base of the head.

Ears (make 2)

Using 3.5mm hook and A, make a magic ring (see page 44).
Round 1: 1 ch, 6 dc into centre of the ring (6 sts).
Round 2: 2 dc in each st (12 sts).
Rounds 3–4: Work 2 rounds straight.
Round 5: (2 dc, dc2tog) three times (9 sts). Fasten off.
Flatten ear. Leave a yarn tail to sew to the head.

Head

Using 3.5mm hook and B, make a magic ring.
Round 1: 1 ch, 6 dc into the centre of the ring.
Round 2: 2 dc into each st (12 sts).
Round 3: (1 dc, dc2inc) six times (18 sts).
Round 4: (2 dc, dc2inc) six times (24 sts).
Round 5: (3 dc, dc2inc) six times (30 sts).
Round 6: (4 dc, dc2inc) six times (36 sts).
Round 7: (5 dc, dc2inc) six times (42 sts).
Rounds 8–12: Work 5 rounds straight.
Round 13: (5 dc, dc2tog) six times (36 sts).

Round 14: (4 dc, dc2tog) six times (30 sts).
Round 15: (3 dc, dc2tog) six times (24 sts).
Round 16: (2 dc, dc2tog) six times (18 sts).
Round 17: (1 dc, dc2tog) six times (12 sts).
Round 18: (dc2tog) six times (6 sts).
Fasten off. Leave a yarn tail to sew to the body.

Using the photograph as a guide, position the eyes on the face.
With a tapestry needle and black embroidery thread, use satin stitch to embroider a small triangle for the nose and then use a back stitch to create a line below the nose (see page 52). Sew the ears firmly to the top of the head.

Arms (make 2)

Using 3.5mm hook and A, make a magic ring.
Round 1: 1 ch, 6 dc into the centre of the ring.
Round 2: (1 dc, dc2inc) three times (9 sts).
Round 3: (2 dc, dc2inc) three times (12 sts).
Rounds 4–16: Work 13 rounds straight.
Fasten off. Leave a yarn tail to sew to the base of the head.

Making up

Stuff the head firmly. Using a tapestry needle, weave the tail of yarn through the last dc sts of the round of the head and gather hole together at the neck edge. Stuff the arms firmly and fold in half widthways at the top of the arms. Sew them to the base of the head near the neck edge.

Blanket

Using 3.5mm hook and B, ch 5 sts, sl st in first ch to form a loop.

Round 1: 3 ch, 2 tr in loop, 3 ch, (3 tr, 3 ch), rep twice more, sl st in 3 ch (4 tr clusters).

Round 2: Change to A, attach yarn to any 3 ch sp, 3 ch, 2 tr in ch sp, 3 ch, 3 tr, 1 ch, (3 tr, 3 ch, 3 tr, 1 ch) in next ch sp three times, sl st in 3 ch (8 tr clusters).

Round 3: Change to B, attach yarn to any 3 ch sp, 3 ch, 2 tr in ch sp, 3 ch, 3 tr, 1 ch, (3 tr, 1 ch) in next ch sp, *(3 tr, 3 ch, 3 tr, 1 ch) in next 3 ch sp, (3 tr, 1 ch) in next ch sp; rep from * twice more, sl st in 3 ch (12 tr clusters).

Continue increasing the granny square in this manner, working in alternate colours.

Work until you have 48 treble clusters ending with a row in A.

Rounds 13–14: Sl st across 2 sts to corner ch sp, 1 ch, (2 dc, 1 ch, 2 dc) into sp, 1 dc into each tr and 1 dc into every 1 ch, (2 dc, 1 ch, 2 dc) into every 3 ch sp, sl st into 1 ch at beg of round.

Fasten off and weave in ends.

Your granny square will measure approximately 10¼in (26cm) square. Gently block the granny square. Fasten off and weave in ends.

Finishing

Sew the head firmly to the centre of the blanket.

Festival Bag

This fun bag has the fresh appeal of boho chic. Surprisingly capacious, it is ideal for storing anything from essentials for a weekend trip to your towel and swimsuit for a trip to the beach.

Finished size

16½in (42cm) wide and 21½in (54cm) long including handles

You will need

- Hayfield Bonus DK, 100% acrylic (306yd/280m per 100g ball):
  1 x 100g ball 887 Bright Pink (A)
  1 x 100g ball 961 White (B)
  1 x 100g ball 992 Pink (C)
  1 x 100g ball 824 Azure (D)
  1 x 100g ball 819 Bright Lemon (E)
  1 x 100g ball 886 Bright Green (F)
- 3.5mm (UK9:USE/4) crochet hook
- 4mm (UK8:USG/6) crochet hook
- 2 x D-shaped bamboo bag handles
- Tapestry needle

Tension

Tension is not essential for this project, but each square is approximately 6 x 6in (15 x 15cm) using a 4mm hook.

Basic square (make 13)

Using 4mm hook and A, ch 4 sts, sl st in first ch to form a loop.

Round 1: 3 ch, 2 tr in loop, 3 ch, (3 tr, 3 ch), rep twice more, sl st in 3 ch (4 tr clusters).

Round 2: Change to B, attach yarn to any 3 ch sp, (3 ch, 2 tr, 3 ch, 3 tr, 1 ch) in ch sp, (3 tr, 3 ch, 3 tr, 1 ch) in next ch sp three times, sl st in 3 ch (8 tr clusters).

Round 3: Change to C, attach yarn to any 3 ch sp, (3 ch, 2 tr, 3 ch, 3 tr, 1 ch) in ch sp, (3 tr, 1 ch) in next ch sp, *(3 tr, 3 ch, 3 tr, 1 ch) in next 3 ch sp, (3 tr, 1 ch) in next ch sp; rep from * twice more, sl st in 3 ch (12 tr clusters).

Round 4: Change to D, attach yarn to any 3 ch sp, (3 ch, 2 tr, 3 ch, 3 tr, 1 ch) in ch sp, (3 tr, 1 ch) in next 2 ch sp, *(3 tr, 3 ch, 3 tr, 1 ch) in next 3 ch sp, (3 tr, 1 ch) in next 2 ch sp; rep from * twice more, sl st in 3 ch (16 tr clusters).

Round 5: Change to E, attach yarn to any 3 ch sp, (3 ch, 2 tr, 3 ch, 3 tr, 1 ch) in ch sp, (3 tr, 1 ch) in next 3 ch sp, *(3 tr, 3 ch, 3 tr, 1 ch) in next 3 ch sp, (3 tr, 1 ch) in next 3 ch sp; rep from * twice more, sl st in 3 ch (20 tr clusters).

Round 6: Change to F, attach yarn to any 3 ch sp, (3 ch, 2 tr, 3 ch, 3 tr, 1 ch) in ch sp, (3 tr, 1 ch) in next 4 ch sp, *(3 tr, 3 ch, 3 tr, 1 ch) in next 3 ch sp, (3 tr, 1 ch) in next 4 ch sp; rep from * twice more, sl st in 3 ch (24 tr clusters).

Fasten off and weave in ends. Complete 13 squares using a combination of different colours.

Half squares (make 2)

Using 4mm hook and A, ch 4 sts, sl st in first ch to form a loop.

Row 1: 4 ch, 3 tr in loop, 3 ch, 3 tr, 1 ch, 1 tr. Fasten off (2 tr clusters).

Row 2: Change to B, attach yarn to 4 ch sp, (4 ch, 3 tr, 1 ch) in same ch sp, (3 tr, 3 ch, 3 tr, 1 ch) in next 3 ch sp, (3 tr, 1 ch, 1 tr) in last ch sp. Fasten off (4 tr clusters).

Row 3: Change to C, attach yarn to 4 ch sp, (4 ch, 3 tr, 1 ch) in same ch sp, (3 tr, 1 ch) in next ch sp, (3 tr, 3 ch, 3 tr, 1 ch) in next 3 ch sp, (3 tr, 1 ch) in next ch sp, (3 tr, 1 ch, 1 tr) in last ch sp. Fasten off (6 tr clusters).

Row 4: Change to D, attach yarn to 4 ch sp, (4 ch, 3 tr, 1 ch) in same ch sp, (3 tr, 1 ch) in next 2 ch sp, (3 tr, 3 ch, 3 tr, 1 ch) in next 3 ch sp, (3 tr, 1 ch) in next 2 ch sp, (3 tr, 1 ch, 1 tr) in last ch sp. Fasten off (8 tr clusters).

Finishing

Weave in ends and block the squares and half squares. Using the diagram as a guide, join the squares together using yarn A by placing a sl st in the back loop of each st in each square.

Top side edging

Round 1: Using 3.5mm hook and A, attach yarn to the corner of a square at the edge of the bag with a sl st, 1 ch, 1 dc into each st and each ch of 1 ch sp. Work down one side of the top edge of the bag and then up the other side.
Repeat for the second side.

Bag handle attachments (make 2)

Round 1: With RS facing and using 3.5mm hook and A, attach yarn to the corner of a square at the right on one side of the bag with a sl st, 3 ch, 2 tr into 3 ch sp, 1 tr in the top on next 3 tr sts, 1 tr in ch sp, 1 tr in next 2 tr sts, 1 tr in the top of seam, working across the top of the half square; 2 tr in each of the ch sp (with 1 tr in space at base of central tr cluster), 1 tr in the top of seam, 1 tr in next 2 tr sts, 1 tr in ch sp, 1 tr in next 3 tr sts and 3 tr into 3 ch sp, turn (37 sts).
Rounds 2–4: Ch 3, 1 tr into each st along edge, turn (37 sts).
Wrap the attachments over the bag handle and sew securely on the inside of the bag.

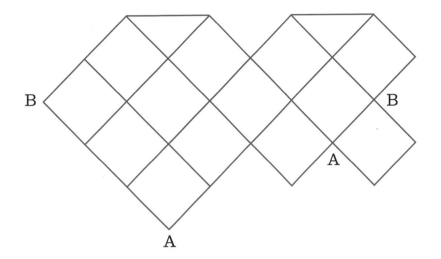

Fingerless Mittens

These fingerless mittens are so simple to make you could crochet a pair to stash in the pockets of every coat you own. They would also make a perfect personalized gift for a treasured friend.

Finished size

3¾in (9.5cm) wide and 6in (15cm) long

You will need

- Debbie Bliss Baby Cashmerino, 55% wool, 33% acrylic, 12% cashmere (137yd/125m per 50g ball):
  1 x 50g ball 001 Primrose (A)
  1 x 50g ball 101 Ecru (B)
  1 x 50g ball 026 Duck Egg (C)
  1 x 50g ball 012 Silver (D)
- 3.5mm (UK9:USE/4) crochet hook
- Tapestry needle

Tension

Tension is not essential for this pattern, but each square motif is approximately 3½ x 3½in (9 x 9cm).

Note

You will need to make two square motifs for this design. You will then add on sections of crochet worked in rows to form the mittens.

Square (make 2)

Round 1: Using 3.5mm hook and A, ch 4 sts, join with a sl st to form a ring.

Round 2: Ch 3 (this counts as first tr), 11 tr into ring, sl st into third ch at beg of round (12 sts). Fasten off.

Round 3: Attach yarn B between any two tr sts, 3 ch (counts as 1 tr), 1 tr into same sp, *2 tr between next 2 sts; rep from * to end, join with a sl st into third of 3 ch. Fasten off.

Round 4: Attach yarn C in sp between any 2 tr groups, 3 ch (counts as first tr), 2 tr into same sp, *3 tr between next 2 tr groups; rep from * to end, join with a sl st into third of 3 ch. Fasten off.

Round 5: Attach yarn D in between any 3 tr groups, 3 ch (counts as first tr) (2 tr, 3 ch, 3 tr) into sp, *1 ch, (3 htr, 1 ch in sp between next two 3 tr groups) twice, (3 tr, 3 ch, 3 tr) between next two 3 tr groups; rep from * twice, 1 ch (3 htr, 1 ch in sp between next two 3 tr groups) twice, join with a sl st into third of 3 ch.

Round 6: Sl st across 2 sts to corner ch sp, 1 ch, (2 dc, 1 ch, 2 dc) into sp, 1 dc into each st and 1 dc into every 1 ch, (2 dc, 1 ch, 2 dc) into every 3 ch sp, sl st into 1 ch at beg of round. Fasten off and weave in ends.

Palm

Row 1: Using 3.5mm hook and D, attach yarn to any 1 ch on the corner of the square with a sl st, 1 ch, 1 dc in each dc and ch, turn (21 sts).

Row 2: 1 ch, 1 dc in each dc, turn (21 sts).

Rows 3–25: Work 23 rows straight. Fasten off.

Left Mitten
Top

Make sure you are looking at your work with the square to the right and the palm dc rows to the left of the square. You will now work the top edging of the mitten.

Row 1: Using 3.5mm hook and D, attach yarn to any 1 ch on the corner of the square with a sl st, 1 ch, work 39 dc evenly along square and side of the palm, turn (39 sts).

Row 2: 1 ch, 1 dc in each dc, turn (39 sts).

Row 3: 1 ch, 1 dc at base of ch, 1 dc, *miss 1 dc, 4 tr in next st, miss 1 dc, sl st in next st, rep from * to last st, 1 dc. Fasten off (9 shell clusters).

Cuff

Turn your work around to ensure the palm crochet is now to the right of the square. You will now work the cuff edging along the base of the mitten.

Row 1: Using 3.5mm hook and D, attach yarn to any st on the corner of the dc palm crochet with a sl st, 1 ch, work 39 dc evenly along side of the palm and square, turn (39 sts).

Rows 2–4: 1 ch, 1 dc in each dc, turn (39 sts).

Row 5: 4 ch, miss st at base of ch, *miss 1 dc, 1 tr in next st; rep from * to end, turn.

Row 6: 1 ch, *1 dc in top of tr, 1 dc in ch sp; rep from * to end, 1 dc in top of third ch, turn (39 sts).

Rows 7–8: 1 ch, 1 dc in each dc, turn (39 sts).

Row 9: 1 ch, 1 dc at base of ch, 1 dc, *miss 1 dc, 4 tr in next st, miss 1 dc, sl st in next st, rep from * to last st, 1 dc (9 shell clusters).

Fasten off.

Right Mitten
Top

Make sure you are looking at your work with the square to the left and the palm dc rows to the right of the square. You will now work the top edging of the mitten.

Row 1: Using 3.5mm hook and D, attach yarn to any st on the corner of the dc palm crochet with a sl st, 1 ch, work 39 dc evenly along side of the palm and square, turn (39 sts).

Row 2: 1 ch, 1 dc in each dc, turn (39 sts).

Row 3: 1 ch, 1 dc at base of ch, 1 dc, *miss 1 dc, 4 tr in next st, miss 1 dc, sl st in next st; rep from * to last st, 1 dc. Fasten off (9 shell clusters).

Cuff

Turn your work around to ensure the palm crochet is now to the left of the square.

You will now work the cuff edging along the base of the mitten.

Row 1: Using 3.5mm hook and D, attach yarn to any 1 ch on the corner of the square with a sl st, 1 ch, work 39 dc evenly along square and side of the palm, turn (39 sts).

Rows 2–4: 1 ch, 1 dc in each dc, turn (39 sts).

Row 5: 4 ch, miss st at base of ch, *miss 1 dc, 1 tr in next st; rep from * to end, turn.

Row 6: 1 ch, *1 dc in top of tr, 1 dc in ch sp; rep from * to end, 1 dc in top of third ch, turn (39 sts).

Rows 7–8: 1 ch, 1 dc in each dc, turn (39 sts).

Row 9: 1 ch, 1 dc at base of ch, 1 dc, *miss 1 dc, 4 tr in next st, miss 1 dc, sl st in next st; rep from * to last st, 1 dc (9 shell clusters).

Fasten off.

Finishing

Weave in all ends.

You will now attach the side seams together of each mitten allowing a hole in the seam for the thumb (see diagram).

Left mitten

With RS together with the back of the granny square facing you, the top of the mitten should be to your right and the cuff should be on the left. Using D, attach yarn with a sl st through both layers at the base of the shell row, 1 ch, 5 dc, working just into the back palm material on the right side, work 12 sl sts, working through both layers of the mitten, 12 dc. Fasten off and weave in ends.

Right mitten

With RS together with the back of the granny square facing you, the top of the mitten should be to your left and the cuff should be on the right. Using D, attach yarn with a sl st through both layers at the base of the shell row, 1 ch, 12 dc, working just into the back palm material on the right side, work 12 sl sts, working through both layers of the mitten, 5 dc. Fasten off and weave in ends.

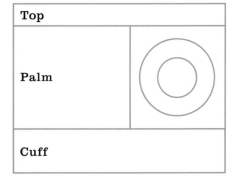

LEFT MITTEN

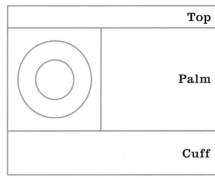

RIGHT MITTEN

Toy Blocks

These colourful toy blocks are as much fun to make as they are to play with. Made in lots of bright and beautiful shades they will be a welcome addition to any nursery.

Finished size

4 x 4 x 4in (10 x 10 x 10cm) cube blocks

You will need

- Stylecraft Classique Cotton 4ply, 100% cotton (199yd/182m per 50g ball):

  1 x 50g ball 3672 Poppy (A)

  1 x 50g ball 3662 Sunflower (B)

  1 x 50g ball 3663 Soft Lime (C)

  1 x 50g ball 3095 Greek Blue (D)

  1 x 50g ball 3673 Lavender (E)

  1 x 50g ball 3667 Sky Blue (F)

  1 x 50g ball 3689 Lapis (G)

  1 x 50g ball 3094 Fondant (H)

- 3mm (UK11:US–) crochet hook
- 4in (10cm) cubes of upholstery foam
- Tapestry needle

Tension

Tension is not essential for this project, but each square is approximately 4 x 4in (10 x 10cm) using a 3mm hook.

Granny squares

Using 3mm hook and A, ch 4 sts, sl st in first ch to form a loop.

Round 1: 3 ch, 2 tr in loop, 3 ch, (3 tr, 3 ch), rep twice more, sl st in 3 ch (4 tr clusters).

Round 2: Change to B, attach yarn to any 3 ch sp, (3 ch, 2 tr, 3 ch, 3 tr, 1 ch) in ch sp, (3 tr, 3 ch, 3 tr, 1 ch) in next ch sp three times, sl st in 3 ch (8 tr clusters).

Round 3: Change to C, attach yarn to any 3 ch sp, (3 ch, 2 tr, 3 ch, 3 tr, 1 ch) in ch sp, (3 tr, 1 ch) in next ch sp, *(3 tr, 3 ch, 3 tr, 1 ch) in next 3 ch sp, (3 tr, 1 ch) in next ch sp; rep from * twice more, sl st in 3 ch (12 tr clusters).

Round 4: Change to D, attach yarn to any 3 ch sp, (3 ch, 2 tr, 3 ch, 3 tr, 1 ch) in ch sp, (3 tr, 1 ch) in next 2 ch sp, *(3 tr, 3 ch, 3 tr, 1 ch) in next 3 ch sp, (3 tr, 1 ch) in next 2 ch sp; rep from * twice more, sl st in 3 ch (16 tr clusters).

Round 5: Change to E, attach yarn to any 3 ch sp, (3 ch, 2 tr, 3 ch, 3 tr, 1 ch) in ch sp, (3 tr, 1 ch) in next 3 ch sp, *(3 tr, 3 ch, 3 tr, 1 ch) in next 3 ch sp, (3 tr, 1 ch) in next 3 ch sp; rep from * twice more, sl st in 3 ch (20 tr clusters).

Fasten off and weave in ends. Make another square in this pattern, reversing the colour sequence.

Mitred squares

Using 3mm hook and G, ch 4 sts, sl st in first ch to form a loop.

Round 1: 3 ch, 2 tr in loop, 3 ch, (3 tr, 3 ch), rep twice more, sl st in 3 ch (4 tr clusters).

Now work in rows.

Row 2: Change to D, attach yarn to any 3 ch sp, 3 ch, 2 tr in same ch sp, 1 ch, (3 tr, 3 ch, 3 tr) in corner 3 ch sp, 1 ch, 3 tr in next 3 ch sp, turn.

Row 3: Ch 4, 3 tr in next 1 ch sp, 1 ch, (3 tr, 3 ch, 3 tr) in next corner 3 ch sp, 1 ch, 3 tr in next 1 ch sp, 1 ch, 1 tr in third of 3 ch from previous row, turn. Break off yarn D.

Row 4: Change to F, attach yarn to 4 ch sp, 3 ch, 2 tr in same ch sp, 1 ch, 3 tr in next 1 ch sp, 1 ch, (3 tr, 3 ch, 3 tr) in next corner 3 ch sp, 1 ch, 3 tr in next 1 ch sp, 1 ch, 3 tr in next 1 ch sp, turn.

Row 5: Ch 4, (3 tr in next 1 ch sp, 1 ch) twice, (3 tr, 3 ch, 3 tr) in next corner 3 ch sp, 1 ch, (3 tr in next 1 ch sp, 1 ch) twice, 1 tr in third of 3 ch from previous row, turn. Break off yarn F.

Row 6: Change to H, attach yarn to 4 ch sp, 3 ch, 2 tr in same ch sp, 1 ch, (3 tr in next 1 ch sp, 1 ch) twice (3 tr, 3 ch, 3 tr) in next corner 3 ch sp, 1 ch, (3 tr in next 1 ch sp, 1 ch) twice, 3 tr in next 1 ch sp, turn.

Row 7: Ch 4, (3 tr in next 1 ch sp, 1 ch) three times (3 tr, 3 ch, 3 tr) in next corner 3 ch sp, 1 ch, (3 tr in next 1 ch sp, 1 ch) three times, 1 tr in third of 3 ch from previous row, turn. Break off yarn H.

Row 8: Change to C, attach yarn to 4 ch sp, 3 ch, 2 tr in same ch sp, 1 ch, (3 tr in next 1 ch sp, 1 ch) three times, (3 tr, 3 ch, 3 tr) in next corner 3 ch sp, 1 ch, (3 tr in next 1 ch sp, 1 ch) three times, 3 tr in next 1 ch sp, turn.

Row 9: Ch 4, (3 tr in next 1 ch sp, 1 ch) four times (3 tr, 3 ch, 3 tr) in next corner 3 ch sp, 1 ch, (3 tr in next 1 ch sp, 1 ch) four times, 1 tr in third of 3 ch from previous row, turn. Break off yarn C.

Weave in ends.

Make another square in this pattern, reversing the colour sequence.

Bear square (make 2)

Using 3mm hook and B, ch 4 sts, sl st in first ch to form a loop.

Round 1: Ch 3, 15 tr in loop, sl st in 3 ch (16 tr).

Round 2: Ch 3, 1 tr in st at base of ch, 2 tr in each tr, sl st in 3 ch (32 tr).

Round 3: (Ears) Work in front loop only, 1 ch, 1 dc in next tr, (1 htr, 1 tr, 1 htr) in next tr, 1 dc in next tr, 5 sl st, 1 dc in next tr, (1 htr, 1 tr, 1 htr) in next tr, 1 dc in next tr, 1 sl st. Fasten off.

Round 4: Change to A, attach yarn to the back loop of the first ear st (1 htr, 1 tr, 1 htr), (5 ch, 1 dtr), 1 dtr in next back loop, 1 tr in back loop of next 5 sl st, 1 dtr in back loop of next st, (1 dtr, 2 ch, 1 dtr) in back loop of next st, 1 dtr in back loop of next st, * 5 tr, 1 dtr, (1 dtr, 2 ch, 1 dtr), 1dtr; rep from * 5 tr, 1 dtr in next back loop, sl st in third of 5 ch (36 sts).

Rounds 5–6: Ch 3, 1 tr in next tr, (1 tr, 2 ch 1 tr) in each ch sp, 1 tr into top of each tr around.

Fasten off and weave in ends. Using some black embroidery thread and the photograph as a guide, embroider two eyes, a nose and a smile onto the bear's face (see page 52).

Finishing

Weave in ends and block each of your squares. Using the diagram as a guide, join the squares together using yarn A by placing a sl st in the back loop of each st in each square. Insert the foam cube before joining the final square.

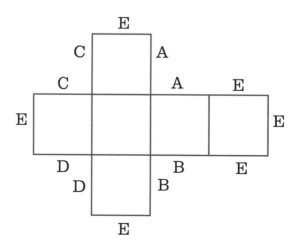

Striped Beret

This jaunty beret uses the same principle as a circular granny
square technique, but introduces the bobble stitch.
When worked in stripes you can create a nautical look.

Finished size

Beret fits an adult female and measures 21¼in (54cm) in circumference

You will need

- MillaMia Naturally Soft Merino, 100% wool (137yd/125m per 50g ball):
  2 x 50g balls 106 Ink Blue (A)
  1 x 50g ball 124 Snow (B)
  1 x 50g ball 168 Butterscotch (C)
- 4mm (UK8:USG/6) crochet hook
- Tapestry needle
- Pompom maker 2½in (6.5cm) in diameter

Tension

Tension is not essential for this project, but there are 8 bobbles per 4in (10cm).

Notes

Beg bobble: 3 ch, (yrh and insert hook in 1 ch sp, yrh and draw a loop through, yrh and draw through first 2 loops on hook) three times all in the same 1 ch sp, yrh and draw a loop through all 4 loops on hook.

1 bobble: (yrh and insert hook in 1 ch sp, yrh and draw a loop through, yrh and draw through first 2 loops on hook) four times all in the same 1 ch sp, yrh and draw a loop through all 5 loops on hook.

Dec 1 bobble: (yrh and insert hook in 1 ch sp, yrh and draw a loop through, yrh and draw through first 2 loops on hook) four times all in the same 1 ch sp, rep in next ch sp, yrh and draw a loop through all 9 loops on hook.

Beret

Round 1: Using 4mm hook and A, ch 4 sts, join with a sl st to form a ring.

Round 2: Ch 3 (this counts as first tr), 11 tr into ring, sl st into third ch at beg of round (12 sts).

Round 3: Beg bobble, 1 ch, *1 bobble in next sp, 1 ch; rep from * 10 times, sl st in top of 3 ch. Fasten off (12 bobbles).

Round 4: Attach yarn B in any ch sp, beg bobble, 1 bobble in same ch sp, *2 bobbles in next ch sp; rep from * 10 times, sl st in top of 3 ch. Fasten off (24 bobbles).

Round 5: Attach yarn A in between any 2 bobbles, beg bobble, 1 ch, *1 bobble, 1 ch; rep from * 22 times, sl st in top of 3 ch. Fasten off (24 bobbles).

Round 6: Attach yarn B in ch sp, beg bobble, 1 bobble in same ch sp, 1 bobble in next ch sp, *2 bobbles in next ch sp, 1 bobble in next ch sp; rep from * 10 times, sl st in top of 3 ch. Fasten off (36 bobbles).

Round 7: Attach yarn A in between any 2 bobbles, beg bobble, 1 ch, *1 bobble, 1 ch; rep from * 34 times, sl st in top of 3 ch. Fasten off (36 bobbles).

Round 8: Attach yarn B in ch sp, beg bobble, 1 bobble in same ch sp, 1 bobble in next 2 ch sp, *2 bobbles in next ch sp, 1 bobble in next 2 ch sp; rep from * 10 times, sl st in top of 3 ch. Fasten off (48 bobbles).

Round 9: Attach yarn A in between any 2 bobbles, beg bobble, 1 ch, *1 bobble, 1 ch; rep from * 46 times, sl st in top of 3 ch. Fasten off (48 bobbles).

Round 10: Attach yarn B in ch sp, beg bobble, 1 bobble in same ch sp, 1 bobble in next 3 ch sp, *2 bobbles in next ch sp, 1 bobble in next 3 ch sp; rep from * 10 times, sl st in top of 3 ch. Fasten off (60 bobbles).

Round 11: Attach yarn A in between any 2 bobbles, beg bobble, 1 ch, *1 bobble, 1 ch; rep from * 58 times, sl st in top of 3 ch. Fasten off (60 bobbles).

Rounds 12–15: Alternating colours to keep patt correct, rep round 11.

Round 16: Attach yarn B in any ch sp, beg dec bobble, 1 ch, (1 bobble in next ch sp, 1 ch) three times, *dec 1 bobble, 1 ch (1 bobble in next ch sp, 1 ch) three times; rep from * 10 times, sl st in top of 3 ch. Fasten off (48 bobbles).

Round 17: Attach yarn A in between any 2 bobbles, beg bobble, 1 ch, *1 bobble, 1 ch; rep from * 46 times, sl st in top of 3 ch. Fasten off (48 bobbles).

Round 18: Attach yarn B in any ch sp, 3 ch, (yrh and insert hook in 1 ch sp, yrh and draw a loop through, yrh and draw through first 2 loops on hook) three times all in the same 1 ch sp, (yrh and insert hook in next 1 ch sp, yrh and draw a loop through, yrh and draw through first 2 loops on hook) four times all in the same ch sp, yrh and draw a loop through all 8 loops on hook, (dec 1 bobble), 1 ch, (1 bobble in next ch sp, 1 ch) twice, *dec 1 bobble, 1 ch (1 bobble in next ch sp, 1 ch) twice; rep from * 10 times, sl st in top of 3 ch (36 bobbles).

Round 19: Attach yarn A, 1 ch, work 1 dc in the top of each bobble and each 1 ch around, sl st in top of ch (72 sts).

Rounds 20–22: Rep round 19.

Round 23: 1 ch, work tbl around, sl st in ch. Fasten off.

Finishing

Weave in all ends. Make a pompom using C (see page 50) and sew securely to the top of the beret.

Sources and resources

Suppliers

The yarns used in these projects should be available from your local yarn or craft store. If you can't find them, try some of the websites shown below.

UK

Black Sheep Wools
Warehouse Studios
Glaziers Lane
Culcheth
Warrington
Cheshire WA3 4AQ
+44 (0)1925 764231
www.blacksheepwools.com

Debbie Bliss Designer Yarns
Units 8–10, Newbridge Industrial Estate
Pitt Street
Keighley
West Yorkshire BD21 4PQ
+44 (0)1535 664222
www.designeryarns.uk.com

Fred Aldous: Art & Craft Supplies
37 Lever Street
Manchester M1 1LW
+44 (0)161 236 4224
www.fredaldous.co.uk

Hobbycraft
Stores nationwide
+44 0330 026 1400
www.hobbycraft.co.uk

John Lewis
Stores nationwide
+44 03456 049 049
www.johnlewis.com

Love Crochet
+44 (0)845 544 2196
www.lovecrochet.com

Stylecraft
Spectrum Yarns
Spa Mill
Slaithwaite
Huddersfield HD7 5BB
+44 (0)1535 609798
www.stylecraft-yarns.co.uk

USA

A.C. Moore Arts & Crafts
Stores nationwide
+1 888 226 6673
www.acmoore.com

Hobby Lobby
Stores nationwide
+1 855 329 7060
www.hobbylobby.com

Michaels
Stores nationwide
1-800-642-4235
www.michaels.com

Books

Cute and Easy Crochet by Nicki Trench
(CICO Books, 2011)

Simple Crochet by Sara Sinaguglia
(Mitchell Beazley, 2012)

Granny Squares by Susan Pinner
(GMC Publications, 2013)

Websites

Attic 24 is a must for all who are new to crochet
www.attic24.typepad.com

Debbie Bliss's books and patterns always inspire me
www.debbieblissonline.com

Jane Crowfoot's site will help you take your crochet
blanket making to a new level
www.janiecrow.co.uk

Vanessa Mooncie has written beautiful crochet books
www.kissysuzuki.com

Pinterest is great for colour combination ideas
www.pinterest.com

Author's acknowledgements

Working on this book has been a team effort. Lots of talented people think about the projects, the patterns and the images so that your experience is good. I would like to thank the wonderful team at GMC, especially my editor Wendy McAngus, who is a dream to work with. Thank you also to Jonathan Bailey, the publisher who trusts me to come up with appealing projects. Thanks must also go to the wonderful photographer, Emma Sekhon, the illustrator Martin Woodward, to Manisha Patel for the overall design and Nicola Hodgson for the copy editing. Thank you also to Jude Roust, who did a wonderful job checking the patterns.

Thank you to my friend Sue Sherry, who is always my first port of call, checking my ideas and especially my maths. She has very beady eyes.

Thank you to my friend and inspiration, Debbie Bliss.

I would like to thank a number of yarn producers and retailers for their support. Thanks to Stylecraft Ltd and the team at Spa Mill – Annabell, Juliet, Sophie and Anna – who generously donated many of the yarns for the blankets. Thanks to Sara and the team at Black Sheep Wools for their ongoing support and for running a fab yarn shop. Thanks also to the team at LoveKnitting, who have also been generous with their yarns, especially the Paintbox cotton.

I am grateful that my family always encourages me to create and puts up with so much yarn in our lives. For this book, Benjamin and Robert have been my quality controllers and my timekeepers – I love you and thank you for your cheerleading.

The publishers would also like to thank Claire and Ismai for modelling.

Index

To order a book, or to request
a catalogue, contact:
GMC Publications Ltd
Castle Place, 166 High Street, Lewes,
East Sussex, BN7 1XU
United Kingdom
Tel: +44 (0)1273 488005
www.gmcbooks.com